Our Lady,
Queen of the Highways

Our Lady,
Queen of the Highways

A memoir

by

TIM COONAN

Adelaide Books
New York / Lisbon
2022

OUR LADY, QUEEN OF THE HIGHWAYS
A memoir
By Tim Coonan

Copyright © by Tim Coonan
Cover design © 2022 Adelaide Books

Published by Adelaide Books, New York / Lisbon
adelaidebooks.org
Editor-in-Chief
Stevan V. Nikolic

For any information, please address Adelaide Books
at info@adelaidebooks.org
or write to:
Adelaide Books
244 Fifth Ave. Suite D27
New York, NY, 10001

ISBN: 978-1-958419-05-2

Printed in the United States of Americ

For my parents, who showed me the Grand Canyon

And for Bridget and Carrie,
whom Cathy and I took to the Grand Canyon

Tim Coonan

Contents

Tim Coonan

Foreword

All my life, I pretty much had the same relationship with my mom, one focused on, or at least represented by, my hair. I grew up, matriculated, in the 1970s, which means I had a pretty bad haircut for most of that era. And beyond, actually. I tended to wear my hair fairly long, and sometimes still do. Go too long between haircuts. In fact, I might have had a bad haircut for most of my life. You could put that on my headstone: he had a bad haircut most of his life. But this I know to be true. If ever I wanted to please my mom, all I had to do was walk through the door with a recent, and short, haircut. And this has been true all my life! At age 60, walking through the door of my parents' house with a recent haircut produced the same effect as it had for decades. "Oh, Tim," she'd say, "I really like it when you get your hair cut."

I appreciate the consistency here. She was the same way about jackets, keeping warm. As adults – older adults! – Dan and I might be headed downtown for a drink, and she'd say, "Are you two going to be warm enough? Do you have jackets?" I love that. Maybe it's just true that you worry about your kids all your life.

In the end, we worried about her. We watched dementia tighten its grip on her, never easing up, causing her to fade. She passed in July 2020, and life has irrevocably changed for us, the family unit, intact for 60-plus years, now altered. Mom clung to life tenaciously. She lasted much longer in hospice care than expected; the hospice nurse had never seen anything like it, but, as she pointed out, she had never encountered an Irish mom before. I personally think Mom held on because she had to make sure all her kids, who spent the week together, for the first time in years, had worked out everything there was to work out among them.

I'm sorry Mom isn't here to read this. She was a voracious reader, an English teacher by nature and profession. She would not have appreciated the occasional f-bombs, of course. Profanity and the like in movies and books? "I don't think that was really necessary, do you?"

But I'm also sorry because this book – and I hesitate to even call it that, the term book conferring much more legitimacy, more heft, than this perhaps warrants – is really a love letter to my parents, a giant thank-you card to them, for taking us on these trips and thus lifting the veil, prying off the lid to this big country for us. It's a love letter to my siblings, as well. We may never have been more together as a family, both literally and emotionally, than we were on these trips, when it was us in a station wagon, taking on this country together. Maybe that's why Mom hung on, so we could regain this type of closeness.

These trips were well-documented, as was our family life in general. Dad took tons of pictures, which didn't just lay around, but went into albums, labelled by year, and, being the organized engineer that he is, were placed in order on the shelf of the closet in the front hall. They are a great primary source, as the historians would say. Later Dad made copies of pictures from our trips and gave us each an album chronicling them: "Across America With the Coonans". I've managed to scan some of these original trip pictures to illustrate this, and like other pictures from the past, they just take you back immediately. To the shores of Lake Springfield and Lake Quinsigamond. To the steps of the

Lincoln Memorial. An empty Notre Dame football stadium, in the summer.

But ironically, there are virtually NO pictures of the eight of us from these trips. Dad was always taking the pictures, and was rarely in them. Aunt Pat had a 35mm camera and took a great picture in 1969 of seven of us (Dennis would be born the following May). And if one of these trips was the high-water mark for us, it may have been the 1972 trip. Terry and I were 13, Dan, 10; Katie was 7, Nora, 4 and Dennis 2. No teenage angst, or even 70s long hair, for anyone, yet. Our lives were all possibility at that point; no doors had been closed to any of us. Let's go see the country.

"You just gotta have a program!" one particular Dodger Stadium program seller would cry as we entered the game. Because you can't know the players without a program. Besides those players mentioned above, there are a few others you should know about, in case you have trouble following along. I was married to Kayci from 1984-1992. That union produced only cats, and we each took one. Cathy and I were married from 1995-2014, and we had Bridget and Carrie.

I have derived inspiration and even guidance for doing this type of thing from a number of writers, all of whom have shown that you can present the past in a humorous, loving and appreciative manner. These authors include Bill Bryson, Chris Erskine, and Anthony Bourdain, among others. Tom Swegle provided review and encouragement, and great pictures of our Carroll Hall days. Closer to home, my brother Dan has proven to me and others that you don't have to be a professional writer to write, to pen something that is of value. Dan has encouraged me every step of the way, and has provided guidance, insightful and gentle review, and resources for this effort of mine, which is perhaps a puny and inadequate rendering of past events. It is even perhaps drivel, but it's MY drivel. Last, my partner in adventures and life in general, Nell Oliver, has been nothing but supportive and encouraging to me in this somewhat soul-baring effort.

I told my sister Katie that I was writing this, and I tried to describe what it was, exactly. "It's kind of like a memoir," I told her, "though I don't like that term; memoirs are for ex-presidents. This is just what happened."

"Then you should call it that," she said.

Here it is, then. This is what happened. Mostly.

Worcester, Massachusetts, 1969: we sat on Nana's couch for this picture by Aunt Pat. Dad and Mom and, from left, Nora, Katie, Dan, myself and Terry. Dennis would be born the following May.

Divine Protection

Our Lady, Queen of the Highways, pray for us
St. Christopher, be with us

So began every family trip, my dad leading us in that prayer as he drove the station wagon away from our home town. Now, as far as I know, there is no Our Lady, Queen of the Highways. That is not an official appellation for the Virgin Mary, like "Our Lady of Sorrows" or "Our Lady of Guadalupe". I don't know if my dad made that up, or if he got it from somewhere. However, there is also no "Our Lady of Malibu", but that in fact is the name of a Catholic parish in that coastal enclave. Whose schoolkids, I might add, are absolute hellions. I know because I chaperoned an outdoor education trip for my daughter's class, and bunked with the chaperone from OLM. Poor guy. He was up every night dealing with the latest trouble his kids had gotten into. My kids were no trouble at all, and were somewhat in awe of the Ugg-wearing, blonde, free-spirited kids from OLM.

But I digress. The point is, by invoking the good name of OLQH, we had secured divine protection for our Chevy Bel-Air station wagon (and in future years, the Kingswood) and its inhabitants, on our rather ambitious trips, coast-to-coast forays to visit relatives and see America. We made four of these, in 1967, 1969, 1972, and 1976, years that now stand out in my mind like Olympic years or election years do, or years of Dodger World Series victories or Notre Dame national championships, as notating significant and somewhat regular events (granted, the World Series victories and national championships have not been nearly as regular as many of us would have hoped).

**Our route followed the "Mother Road", Route 66/I40, to Illinois.
Sacred places noted on the map.**

Saying the road trip prayer was completely in character for our large Irish-Catholic family, who, for a period of time, knelt and said the Rosary nightly in front of the Virgin Mary figurine on the living room bookcase. A Virgin Mary whose head had been severed several times by balls, which were not allowed in the house.

How Catholic were we? Very. We attended tiny, funky St. Anthony's school in El Segundo, in the shadow of the Standard Oil refinery where my dad worked – when the church windows were open, from the pews you could see, and hear, the massive machinery of the refinery in action, breaking down crude oil and sending steam into the air. The school was set on a hill covered in blacktop. We were toughened by daily football games on asphalt; after recess, Deane DeFontes, the best athlete in our class, would be rinsing the blood off his elbows at the drinking fountain. We boys wore flimsy, white collared shirts over white undershirts, and salt-and-pepper cords which came in three fits: I was always a "slim" and Terry a "husky"; neither of us was a "regular." The girls wore the same flimsy white collared shirts and plaid jumpers, which, by the time we reached the upper grades, looked pretty damned good on some of them. The school was staffed by nuns, who wore habits and were not hesitant to use a ruler on recalcitrant students. And Sister Linda Peters, our fourth-grade teacher, could throw a football farther and more accurately than Deane DeFontes.

The Catholicism into which we were indoctrinated was a 1950's/60's literal version: the Baltimore Catechism with its depiction of a pure soul, a gleaming white milk bottle, contrasting with the impure soul – a milk bottle which was smudged and blackened. There was apparently no non-dairy option for the lactose-intolerant. Our concepts of sin, at that point, were wonderfully simple. Asked for examples of what might be a mortal sin, Fred Curcio offered the following: "Step on a rosary? Throw a rock in a church?" Instead of Halloween costumes we came to school dressed as saints for the saint parade. Terry and I favored the warrior saints, like dragon-slaying St. George or St. Martin of Tours; for those costumes we got to bring a lance or a foil-covered cardboard sword and shield to school. Every month we collected money to feed the Pagan Babies, whom we got to "name"; one month the boys in the class named a Pagan Baby after Roman Gabriel, then quarterback of the Los Angeles Rams (I sincerely hope that there's a guy in equatorial Africa with the name of Roman Gabriel). Probably the highlight of our school week was Hot Dog Day. I never ate the hot dog, just the bun; gave the hot dog to Terry. Little wonder I was a slim and he was a husky.

15

First day of first grade, 1965. Patent-leather shoes, etc., with childhood friend Dena.

Sure, they were chaste and holy and pure and all that, but the warrior saints kicked some ass, too. St. Martin of Tours, left, and St. George.

As a first-grader, I remember that the eighth-grade boys looked huge. They were practically grown men, in my eyes; I'm sure they came to school - maybe even drove themselves - with cigarette packs rolled up in their sleeves and with five-o'clock shadows on their faces. By fifth grade we were card-carrying members of Mrs. Michelson's Dominic Savio Club, with a devotion to that boy saint marked by a promise to remain celibate and say the Rosary daily. For the rest of our lives. When my sister Katie had Mrs. Michelson, she would occasionally have Katie watch the class while Mrs. Michelson took a cigarette break in the supply room next door. By eighth grade we boys were the lead altar servers – this was well before girls broke that barrier – and Bob Gilbert was sampling the altar wine in the back of the sacristy. I was too scared to; was that a mortal sin?

Granted, it sometimes seems as though Catholicism and drinking went hand-in-hand. Some dads (but not mine!) were members of the local Knights of Columbus and would day-drink at the local K of C hall while we boys played pool and ping-pong there. And then there was Monsignor Maddox, known to play cards with local parishioner families on "Vatican Hill", a street where many Catholic families lived, and sometimes he had trouble getting back to the rectory after a night of cards and Scotch.

How Catholic were we? Dad and Uncle Ted went to Notre Dame, as did three of us kids. My twin brother Terry became a Catholic priest. Then he un-became a priest. But again, I digress. We'll get to Terry, and everyone else, all in good time. These trips, and the places we visited, were some of the most formative experiences of our youth, and, at least in my case, likely set me on the course I would take later in life. A sense of place.

These trips – what an undertaking! Six kids (eventually) in the station wagon. Heading to the East Coast. Why?? For one, to see our relatives, my dad's folks in Massachusetts and my mom's in Illinois. Because, God forbid, we certainly weren't going to FLY back there. Nobody did that! It was too expensive! Nowadays people fly everywhere, at the drop of a hat. Heck, my first plane flight was pretty much when I left for college. According to Mom, in 1967 they had just bought the station wagon, and this was an excuse to use it. But I'm trying to imagine the conversations my parents must have had when planning these trips. My dad saying, "Kay, why don't we pack the kids in the station wagon and drive to the East Coast, and take a month to do it?" And my mom saying, "Are you fucking kidding me?!!" Actually, I can't imagine my mom saying that. Their generation didn't sling f-bombs around as much as successive generations do. Yes, we fly, and we drop f-bombs, at the drop of a hat. But they didn't. Heck, they didn't even argue! I can remember only one time when my Dad raised his voice to my Mom. They had taken us to Mount Waterman to sled in the snow one winter Sunday. Now, the old station wagon – the 1966 Chevy Bel Air, the Bomb, as we affectionately called it when we drove it to high school – was heavy as fuck (sorry, there I go again) but was certainly not four-wheel drive. My Dad was backing up to turn around up there, and the back end was heading toward a snowbank or rock or small child or some such obstacle, which my Mom informed him of, and he turned to her and said, "Damn it, Kay, I can see that!". Swear to God, that was the only time in 60-plus years that I heard a curse word or a raised voice. Though Mom always claimed she swore in Gaelic – can't say I ever heard it. Exemplary marriage. But we'll get to that.

Good lord, how did they plan for such a trip? My dad said he was a basket case as he packed the car and made sure all the tires were full, etc. We all shared suitcases, the big, brown leather type. My dad eventually bought a luggage rack for the top of the station wagon, because after a while one or two kids had to be in the "way back". A prized position in the car, fought over for sure, because you could recline back there, get comfortable with a book. One trip I was reading the Lord of the Rings trilogy back there. What did we need? Swimsuits. Baseball gloves. Baseball, bat. Caps. There were apple boxes full of food – because we certainly weren't going to buy lunch or breakfast – and a white Styrofoam cooler, which just might still be in my Dad's garage. Dan remembers that the cooler and lid would squeak as we drive, incessantly, and we just got used to that sound, a sound of vacation. The green Coleman thermos jug we had is certainly still in my Dad's garage, high up on a wooden shelf; it was filled with ice and water for the day's drive. There was a white plastic cup with a sloped side that fit inside the screwtop, and I can still picture taking that out and filling it with icewater from the spigot. Can still taste it. This was well before Nalgene water bottles or the now-ubiquitous HydroFlasks. How did my parents pack enough stuff for our family for a month on the road? I have no idea.

I find it remarkable that Dad could, and did, take a month off work to do this. No cell phone or email to check in with. And apparently, no problem. Dad was a chemical engineer at the Chevron (nee Standard Oil) refinery in El Segundo, our home town. And I'll tell you this, he valued his vacation time. Taught us to value it, as well. Of course, it DID piss some people off. Sometimes we'd leave for the East Coast before Little League season had ended. Mr. Nichols, manager of the major league Tigers, was not happy that his first and second basemen would be gone for the latter part of the season. I seem to recall that as being a heated discussion after a Little League game. With all the heat coming from Mr. Nichols.

One thing they definitely had going for them was the "Triptik". Prepared by AAA upon request, TripTiks were books of maps which traced your intended route, day by day. They were fascinating, with features listed on foldouts, and there was real sense of accomplishment, of tangible progress, when your drive required you to turn the page to the next map. The Triptik lived in the front seat, in the glove compartment or on the dash, and it was consulted often. That and a AAA guide to the Southwest, or Northeast, with lodging listings. My dad wouldn't make reservations ahead of time, but would call ahead to a motel when we made our afternoon stop for gas. He would disappear into a pay phone booth at the gas station, with his AAA book, and when he reappeared, we only cared about one thing: did it have a pool?

What else did they take? The coffee pot! My mom packed the kitchen percolator coffee pot, and fixed coffee in the morning at the motel. This was well before Starbucks or even complimentary coffee in the room. She would fill a Thermos with it, and pour a cup for my dad throughout the day.

This was high adventure for us kids. We were not the type of family who skied, or camped. Lake cabins, yes. Otherwise our El Segundo summers were marked by riding our bikes around town to Little League, library classes, archery and cooking classes at El Segundo Rec Park, where we also played shuffleboard and paddle tennis and snuck onto the lawn bowling green. The annual trip to Disneyland, pretty much a birthright for Angelenos. Swimming lessons at the El Segundo Plunge – how I hated those! That is still the smell of fear for me – the scent of chlorine when you entered the Plunge and we boys turned to the right, skittering down the dank tunnel leading to the boys changing room. Hanging your towel and clothes on those mesh hangers, which you'd give to the attendant. (Later, I became that attendant - that was my first job! The other attendant stashed Playboys in that desk. A formative experience, to be sure. Barbara Leigh in a breechclout. Is that why I took a Native American anthropology course in college?) The attendant gave you a numbered metal pin you'd attach to your swimsuit. Then taking the mandatory shower and, shivering from fear as well as cold, you'd head up the ramp to the pool, where lifeguards were assigned to torture you, make you put your face in the water. Waiting to graduate from the little pool to the big one. Terry moved on to the big pool before me, much to my embarrassment. Thank God I could see Mom waiting and watching in the stands. And no wonder we occasionally peed in the pool. That's what fear does to you.

Dodger caps at Disneyland

If swimming lessons were the worst thing about growing up in El Segundo, I'll take it. It was – and still is – a sleepy little town insulated from the greater LA area. More Midwestern than SoCal coastal. A great place to grow up. El Segundo is surrounded by the Pacific Ocean to the west, LAX to the north, the Chevron refinery to the south, and the aerospace industry to the east, and had none of the problems that more urban parts of LA had. Barely any crime.

The beloved Stick...and its primary patron.

My brother Terry was pulled over by El Segundo PD for blowing through a stop sign. On his bike. Probably made the police blotter. El Segundo's quaint Main Street boasted the Gay 90s ice cream parlor, certainly the highlight for us kids. A real soda fountain. Were there bad kids in town? Yup. They hung out on Devil's Path, the abandoned railroad spur running into town. Or they were making out on the sand dunes on the west end, where the town ended and the Hyperion Water treatment plant began. It processed sewage for the Los Angeles area, and earned El Segundo the appellation of El Stinko. The surf break there was called Shit Pipe. At that time, in the 1960s, El Segundo had few restaurants, just the ancient, somewhat exotic and therefore somewhat questionable Canton Low (we were not a Chinese food family, except for canned chow mein noodles), and a Chicken Delight ("Don't Cook Tonight; Call Chicken Delight"). Bars were seedy affairs such as the Vapor Trails and the Keg, and our favorite (when we were older), the Stick 'n Stein. The Stick served huge schooners of beer. Dan would always tie a napkin around his to mark it, and several schooners made it out of the Stick and are likely to this day filled with change and sitting on Coonan dressers. Nowadays El Segundo is trendier, with great restaurants and bars, even a brewery, a surf shop, and several distilleries in the old grimy industrial area of Sleepy Hollow. And the Plunge is still there. Not that I have any desire to step into that place.

Sometimes the whole family gathered at the Stick, on special occasions.

We were perhaps primed to travel, open-minded about it, because of the family concept of "taking trails". And here's the Catholic thing again: we were an 8 o'clock Sunday morning Mass family. Like clockwork. This was before evening Masses, which came into being in time for us to appreciate them as teenagers. But back in the day, you had to show up for 8:00 a.m.

Mass, no matter how late you might've stayed out on Saturday night. Dan maintained that was critical to staying in parental good graces: just show up for 8:00 a.m. Mass. Then afterward, Sunday breakfast at home: bacon and eggs, pancakes, French toast. And the Sunday funnies.

UNLESS.

Unless, after leaving Mass and driving down the hill on Grand, we went straight instead of turning left at Center Street.

"Dad, where are we going?!" we'd shout from the back seat.

"We're just taking trails," he'd smile.

We knew better. We were heading to the pancake house in Manhattan Beach. That's what "taking trails" meant. The kids' pancake with a pineapple slice for a mouth and cherry for a nose. Multiple types of syrup (to this day I favor blueberry). My fave, buckwheat pancakes.

So, in a way, heading east was just taking trails to an extreme. We went straight east instead of turning back home. And leaving El Segundo for these trips was a ritual. Car packed, kids on board…when we hit the freeway, that's when Dad would lead us in our road trip prayer. And it wasn't an early start; we left on our trip in the evening. So we could cross the desert at night.

Forty Days and Forty Nights (okay, one night)

We crossed the desert at night! Like the goddam Joad family, but in reverse! No dead grandma strapped to the tailgate, though. We crossed the California desert at night for one reason: to avoid the summertime desert heat. Because we had no air conditioning! The station wagon we drove on our first trip east, in 1967, was that 1966 Chevy Bel-Air. The Bomb. With no air conditioning. But my dad actually BORROWED an air conditioner for the trip. The unit sat on the floor of the car between the driver and passenger, and was more like a humidifier. You'd put ice cubes in it and cold (cooler?) air issued forth, though certainly not strong enough to reach the way back. Upon request, we kids would put ice from the cooler in a cup and pass it forward to Mom, who kept feeding the air conditioner.

So off we went, but the plan was not to drive all night. We'd drive well into the desert, until, around midnight or so, Mom and Dad decided it was time for us to get some sleep. Then we'd pull over to the side of the road somewhere around Amboy or Ludlow, old Route 66 towns that Interstate 40 has long passed by. And then we'd sleep, or try to. In the car or under it. We boys would have sleeping bags stretched out right on the shoulder, somewhat under the car. All night the traffic would whiz by, and we watched the headlights approach and taillights recede, framed by the pavement and the underside of the station wagon. Mom and the girls slept in the car.

The "Bomb" (not called that by our parents). 1966 Chevy Bel-Air. A real tank. Photo, and dent in tailgate, courtesy of Dan.

As the desert sun rose, we'd pile back in the car, sleeping bags and pillows askew, with a feeling of survivor's success. We had gotten through the night and the desert. The morning view was the first we'd have of the strange and somewhat dreaded Mojave Desert, which we had avoided seeing by our nighttime travels. Sunrise in the desert is pretty peaceful, even on a late June morning, on the shoulder of Route 66. The landscape is sparse. The vegetation – scraggly creosote bushes and low-lying bursage – is evenly spaced, with plenty of desert pavement between plants. Geologists love the desert, because the geology is not hidden. Huge alluvial fans spill down from dry, colorful mountain canyons, turning into dry washes, only rarely filled with water, running to road's edge. Not a tree in sight. The heat already shimmering from the road ahead, which in some places runs arrow-straight to the horizon. A forbidding landscape. And one which I would become intimately familiar with, in later years.

A decent chunk of my 30 years as a biologist with the National Park Service was spent at Death Valley, well to the north of I40, a park I had never visited until arriving there in 1987. It was huge! Seven mountain ranges in the park, it's the biggest NPS unit in the lower 48. So much backcountry to explore. During my time there I bought a four-wheel drive vehicle, my beloved red Nissan Pathfinder, and on our off-days my wife Kayci and I would explore the mountain ranges and canyons. At Death Valley I studied desert pupfish and fire ecology and desert bighorn, my second-favorite wildlife species. At Death Valley, the humbling sense of space is unavoidable; in the morning I'd wake up in my NPS house on the west flank of the Greenwater Range, with a view across the saltpan to the 11,000-foot-high Telescope Peak in the Panamints. I got used to that. For a while I didn't think I could live anywhere else that didn't have that sense of space. And that sense of space comes at a price: Death Valley is a long way from anywhere. Every two weeks we'd head either west to Ridgecrest or east to Las Vegas for groceries, either way a two-hour drive.

But I digress…my Death Valley Days lay 20 years in the future for me, as we woke up by the side of the road in 1967. We finished our California desert drive by heading to Needles, just this side of the Colorado River, and our first new state, Arizona. In Needles we had a picnic breakfast under the shade ramadas at Moabi Park, which was like an oasis after our Steinbeck-like nighttime crossing of the desert. Moabi Park became our first real milestone, a sign of progress. In later years I stopped by there, but like many things to which we once assigned value, or steeped in myth, it was not the same…it was a hot, sandy place where jet-skis were putting into the Colorado River. No matter. I'll remember it for the oasis it was.

Moabi Park in Needles, our first picnic breakfast stop.

Crossing the Rubicon.
Er, the Colorado

Crossing the Colorado River at Needles was huge. A new state! The storied Colorado River! The Grand Canyon State! The Welcome to Arizona sign, with its rising sun state flag. Mom and Dad made sure we appreciated the significance of this milestone. It was a strange feeling to not be in California anymore. Instead, Arizona: a fairly landlocked state of rugged beauty, maybe not quite as sparse as the Mojave Desert. Once across the steel bridge spanning the Colorado, I40 jogged north toward Kingman and then east again, across the desert grasslands of the north central part of the state. Past small Route 66 towns such as Peach Springs, Seligman and Ash Fork; in future years I, being a wildlife biologist, would appreciate those lands as great habitat for American pronghorn, one of the fastest land mammals, and I would stop and look for pronghorn herds in that great expanse. Those towns are portals for entry to the Hualapi and Havasupai reservations, home to peoples who have lived on the edge of the Grand Canyon for centuries. The Havasupai provide access to some of the most spectacular parts of the canyon, the magical waterfalls in Havasu Canyon. Years later I made a solo trek to these falls while at a training course at Grand Canyon National Park, and it was an unforgettable experience.

Past those high desert grassland towns the land, and I40, starts climbing higher out of the desert grasslands. After Ash Fork the highway heads toward the high country, the San Francisco Peaks of northern Arizona. The long-dormant volcanic peaks are surrounded by the ponderosa pines of the Coconino National Forest, much like the hair on a tonsured monk's scalp. The initial portal to this high country is Williams, "Gateway to the Grand Canyon", really just a small logging town that boasts a spur railroad track running north to the canyon. Back in the day, before I40 skirted the town, you drove right through it on Route 66. We kids were always impressed by the ads for Rod's Steak House, with its neon heifer above the door. Another steakhouse, the Big Texan in Amarillo, gave you your meal for free if you finished a 72-ounce steak. We never ate there. Cannot imagine.

Then, 30 or so miles to Flagstaff. Flag! City of dreams for me. I would eventually live in Flagstaff while attending grad school at Northern Arizona University, and for a number of years I just wanted to get back to Flag. More on that later. In June of 1967, we were just passing through. The day's driving destination was Gallup, New Mexico, just over the Arizona-New Mexico state line. After Flag, we headed down the mountain the

Katie and Nora at Arizona's Petrified Forest National Park, 1972

other way, to the east, toward New Mexico. Past the two big arrows by the side of the road. Toward Winslow and Holbrook, and the Painted Desert and Petrified Forest, a weird and wonderful stop for us. Again, a barren landscape, and I would have preferred to stay in mountainous Flagstaff; I watched the Peaks receding in the distance, through the back window. But a second new state lay ahead, New Mexico, Land of Enchantment.

We crossed all of Arizona in a day's drive, and it was, for us, a standard vacation day's drive: eight hours and 500 miles. That's still a standard day's drive for me. Drive straight though? 12, 16, 20 hours? No thanks. And I don't know how Dad did it, driving all day on the few hours' sleep he caught in the desert the night before. At that point Mom didn't drive. But she'd pour him an afternoon cup of coffee from the thermos.

On this first full day of driving, our routine had kicked in. Kids, fairly well-behaved, in the middle seat and way back. The youngest kid or baby in the front, between Mom and Dad, on the wide bench front seat those station wagons had. One kid, the second youngest, had to take the "hump" in the middle seat.

We read and listened to AM radio, piped to the back speaker on later models of station wagons. We were amazed to be able to pick up baseball games all across the country. Mom would pull out maybe one car game per day; a tiny chess set, with the pieces attached to the squares by pegs; coloring books; the old drawing pad you drew on with a stylus and erased by lifting the cellophane off the wax pad. Those little puzzles with 16 squares and one empty. Games you had to tilt to get the little ball to sit in the hole. Rest areas occasionally had these kinds of toys in vending machines. But we were not a stop-and-buy-a-snack kind of traveling family. Not even at the ubiquitous Stuckey's roadside stops.

However, in the afternoon, Mom would pull out her ace in the hole: a roll of Lifesavers! How simple life was then: we each got ONE Lifesaver in the afternoon, and we loved it! Mom would open the roll and pass it back, each kid taking one. It was assorted flavors, and some trading went on…I just wanted the pineapple one.

We all had our ways of passing the time. To keep the younger kids entertained, Terry invented a game – the stupidest game ever. Penny in the Hand. He'd have one penny, show it to Katie, say, and then put both hands behind his back. "Which hand is it in?" Terry would tally her right and wrong answers in his notebook. This went on for hours! Dan counted red barns all across the country, keeping a tally in his notebook. Mom says when he'd nap, he'd ask her to count for him, so as not to miss any.

I probably preferred to watch the land roll by. The country went on forever, a brighter and kinder view of Fitzgerald's dark fields of the republic. Telephone poles and fenceposts marking the miles and the hours, with the New World starting just on the other side of that barbed-wire fence. Did I long to climb over that fence and start walking? Is this when I first developed my appreciation for place? All my life, I have viscerally loved places. It affected my choice of college – what a beautiful campus Notre Dame had – and my decision to stay on campus all four years. I chose a grad school based in part on its location. My choice of life's work ended up being protection and stewardship of places. Maybe the seeds were sown by the views from the way back of a station wagon.

In eastern Arizona I40 passed by Lupton, with its ersatz teepees and trading post tucked under a cliff, on to the state line, and the canyons and mesas of New Mexico. It was all certainly a source of wonder for me. The only conceptions I had, up to that point, of the Southwest came from Dad's Frank and Paul stories, told to us when we needed to think about something else, such as when we got stitches; during one such session the doctor asked my Dad to finish the story. He wanted to know how it turned out. In the stories the twin boys always outwitted the outlaw Black Bart, and saved their sisters Barbara and Anne. In reality, Dad had named the boys in the stories after college roommates, and the girls after a college girlfriend. To return the favor, Mom called the socks that Barbara Anne had knitted for my dad "Barbara Anne socks", and we kids wore them to wax the kitchen floor. My only other impressions of the Southwest came from cartoons, such as one on Captain Kangaroo that featured native American dancing in Albuquerque. Or the Roadrunner and Coyote. Or stories in in Open Highway reader series. I was later to become enamored of the Southwest, and spent much time there. We'll get to that. To this day I am thrilled by the sight of Southwestern skies, with their puffy clouds on the horizon, looking like the backdrop in an oil painting.

The Shalimar Inn as it appeared in the 1960s, in a vintage postcard.

As that first afternoon progressed, our thoughts turned to where we would stay that night, and on that first trip, this was surrounded in mystery for us kids. Turned out my dad had chosen the Shalimar Inn in Gallup. We pulled up, with no clue that…it had a pool! And a restaurant! Both saving the long day and raising expectations for every other future motel stay. And we developed a routine for this, as well. Swim first, dinner – out

– later. What a thing to look forward to on every day of vacation. Here's where those dreaded swimming lessons paid off. Terry and I were 8, Danny 5 on that first trip, and we were allowed to go to the pool ourselves. We'd race to the pool. On later trips, the first to jump in was officially "Joe Hefty". We would toss the mini football to each other as we raced off the diving board (yes, every pool had a diving board), making circus catches and scoring TDs for Notre Dame and the Rams. Dad told me the nightly dip in the pool really was restorative for him, after a long day's drive.

Dinner out was special, and something to which we all looked forward. That evening began an endless series of mainly hamburgers ordered in nightly restaurant stops, and what's wrong with that? I love hamburgers. After Little League games, Terry would get a hot dog, and myself a cheeseburger, giving our order to Dad through the dugout fence during the final inning. Occasionally we would swim AFTER dinner, but otherwise we would read (no electronics!) while Mom and Dad packed for the next day's drive. Including still-wet swimsuits. We perfected the execution of the "overnight bag", one bag which held our swimsuits, toiletries, and a change of clothes for all; this saved Dad the trouble of bringing in all the bags, some of which were in the carrier on top of the car. Many of the motels, or motor lodges, we stayed in featured the "Magic Fingers" coin-operated ostensible massage machine attached to the bed. For two quarters you could get a "massage". We never tried it, of course; who had the money to spend on such? When I finally tried it, years later, I was severely disappointed. The thing just basically shook the bed.

We would not sleep in the next day. Or go out for breakfast. No sirree. We were not that type of travel family. My dad's aim was to get out the door by 7:30 or so, and we pretty much made that timetable. On major trips, you could be out the door maybe a half hour after your intended departure and still meet your objective, a guideline I still follow (though that doesn't work when you're trying to catch a flight!). No breakfast in the room, even, though my mom would have brought in the percolator and the big can of Yuban or Folgers, and made coffee for the day's drive. Then we were off, still-sleepy kids and all. Nope, a picnic breakfast was our first stop, doubling as the first chance for kids to get out and play, run off some energy. My parents were strategic masters of the roadside stop. These were usually at the handy rest areas regularly placed on major highways, always with some green space. We boys, and later, Katie, would play whiffle ball or catch, while my mom walked the younger kids.

The traditional breakfast stop in Grants, New Mexico, 1967 (left) and 1969.

Our breakfast stop after a night in Gallup was Grants, home to a volcanic landscape we came to love, and so we repeated breakfast here in later years. Rocks to climb on! We came to love these picnic breakfasts, because they featured those little individual boxes of cereal. Dad, with his penknife, would slit open the box and the wax paper lining, so it looked like a coat opening, and pour the milk in. Pretty cool. We came to realize very quickly that not all the little cereals were equivalent. Some were much more valuable than others. Cocoa Krispies and Rice Honeys were worth fighting over. Cheerios, Wheaties, Special K, not so much.

That day we crossed New Mexico and drove into the panhandle of Texas, staying in Amarillo for the night. Then across Oklahoma and into Missouri, our last night on the road before arriving in Illinois, Land of Lincoln and ancestral home of the McFaddens, Mom's family. In Joplin our lives were changed forever, for the better. It MAY have been the most significant discovery ever on our trips. Topping Notre Dame, Niagara Falls, the Grand Canyon, Washington, even Gettysburg and Cooperstown, as a place bringing about a sea-change in our collective view of the world, and what it could be. In Joplin, we stayed at a Howard Johnson's.

Howard Johnson's! HOJO! That blue building and orange roof! Oddly, those were the colors of the New York Mets. But was there ever a sight so pregnant with possibility, with pure joy waiting to be had? A Howard Johnson's hotel had everything we wanted. Nice rooms, great pool, and a fantastic restaurant that catered to everyone's tastes. And, most importantly, this experience could be had anywhere there was a Howard Johnson's! When we found out there were other Howard Johnson's, we were in heaven. We never wanted to stay anywhere else. The Howard Johnson's advertisements of the day nailed it, with a Tomorrowland, Post-Modern quality that appealed to everyone who wanted to live in a more perfect world.

After swimming, we headed to the restaurant, right on the premises, and our lives were instantly transformed by the menu offerings, many of which became consistent individual orderings. I favored hamburgers, of course, but sometimes ordered the clam strips. Katie ordered the Spready Freddie peanut butter and jelly sandwich; Dan always had the 3D burger and chocolate milk, never wavered on that. Terry favored hot dogs, and at Howard Johnson's the hot dog came on a grilled split roll, East Coast style, something we'd never seen before. The outside of the roll was buttered and grilled, and it was excellent. And it came with its own little round pot of baked beans! From then on Terry ordered that at every Howard Johnson's we stayed at after that. I know that, because Terry kept a detailed journal of our cross-country trip, faithfully recording what everyone in the family ordered for dinner at every restaurant. Terry still has that journal.

The world as it could be. The apex: hot dog served in a buttered and grilled split roll.

Howard Johnson's of course, was known for its ice cream, and back in the day, everyone ordered dessert after dinner. The Joplin Howard Johnson's had a regional specialty going: blueberry milkshakes. I was a huge fan of blueberries, sometimes even requesting a blueberry pie (over a chocolate cake!) on my birthday, and so I ordered it, and it was everything you might think it would be. And it was a singular experience. To this day, I've never seen another blueberry shake offered anywhere.

The land had changed noticeably by the time we were in Missouri. Gone were the hard, clean lines of the Mojave Desert and the big skies, buttes and mesas of the Southwest, even the hardscrabble shrublands of Texas. The land was lusher; trees and green lined the side of the road. You could no longer see the geology. We had gone past John Wesley Powell's 100th meridian, the line separating the arid West from the humid East. The effects of water here were apparent in the lushness. Other effects were more hidden; water had coursed through these limestone lands for millennia, creating massive caves. We visited one of these, Merrimac Caverns, in 1972. It was a real-life Pirates of the Caribbean. The large cavern had been used as an escape route for outlaw Jesse James (a real-life Black Bart!) and his brother, Frank, and the cave featured life-size figures of the two wading in the underground river. Dad remembers the cave being pitch-black when they turned off the lights during the tour. Frank and Jesse had swum out in the dark...the combination of the beautiful and mysterious cave system with real and somewhat heroic criminal elements left a big impression on us boys. We bought postcards showing Frank and Jesse in the cave.

We had a picnic lunch at Merrimac State Park afterward. Bologna sandwiches on white bread (Wonder Bread), of course, or P, B and J, but sometime these picnic lunches featured those little cans of Underwood deviled ham. And orange soda, Orange

Crush, still a guilty pleasure for me. On one of these Merrimac River picnic lunches, Dennis fell into the river! Some fisherman yelled at my dad, who ran down to the water's edge. Then Dennis stood up. The water was only knee deep. Dennis had a fearlessness about water due in part to his protected status as youngest. He would sometimes jump into a hotel pool, trusting that Dad or one of his older brothers would be right beside him when he popped up.

One year, we spent the Fourth of July in Joplin, and Dad remembers fireworks in the hotel parking lot that night. This took some getting used to; our hometown, like many in fire-prone California, outlaws backyard fireworks, and I'm still a little leery of them. In 1969, we watched the Apollo moon landing on a grainy black and white television in Joplin. I felt bad for Michael Collins, who piloted Apollo 11 while Neil Armstrong and Buzz Aldrin walked on the moon. Like all boys of that time period, I was somewhat obsessed with the NASA moon program. The Apollo 11 spacecraft was one of the plastic models I assembled, and proudly displayed on a shelf in the bedroom Terry and I shared.

But we had our own giant leap to take. We crossed the Mississippi River, even more impressive than the Colorado – it took so long to cross! It went on forever! The Big Muddy! Full of boat traffic, barges and cargo going up and down. Life on the Mississippi. Talk about what separated East from West…this was it. We had entered the non-West, the Midwest and East. Where our family had come from. And specifically, we were in beloved Illinois. Mom was home. You can take the girl out of the Midwest…

Land of Lincoln. And McFadden

Illinois was flat. I mean, the whole state seemed pretty much level. It must have SOME topography, of course…part of it drains to the Mississippi, and part to Lake Michigan. But the flat goes on forever, field after field of corn. Which is not a knock on Illinois; I love the place. Ancestral home of the McFaddens and O'Connors, who likely settled it shortly after the glaciers receded. They then graciously allowed the Sauk and the Kickapoo and Pottawatomie peoples to settle there, and also a guy named Lincoln who was from Indiana or Kentucky or somewhere else, both of which are NOT the Land of Lincoln. Only Illinois can claim that. Those receding glaciers left tons of great soil, glacial till that is rich and flat and easily farmed, and still is east of the 100th meridian and so gets adequate rainfall to grow corn and wheat ("Rain will follow the plow" – what? Who came up with that shit? Land speculators, no doubt). The soil here is so rich that it's black from all the organic material. It's world-famous soil. I know that, because in the textbook for my Notre Dame botany class there is a picture of cornfields in MacLean County, Illinois, which supposedly has some of the richest soil in the world. I took note of that as my uncle Joe McFadden and I drove a moving van with Aunt Carol's things in it north through MacLean County to Rockford one cold Thanksgiving. My wife

Cathy's mom, Nan Schwemm, always claimed Illinois sweet corn and tomatoes in late summer couldn't be beat. Can't really argue with those results. Must be the soil.

The venerable house at 411 S. State Street.

Once we crossed the Mississippi we headed for Springfield, state capitol of Illinois and its spiritual center, as well as that of the McFadden world. Coming from the LA area, I found Springfield, supposedly a state capitol, to be small and really neighborhood-like. My grandfather lived not that far from downtown Springfield, where the capitol building and Lincoln's home and law offices were, and you could walk there from his house, along old streets, some of which were still paved with bricks. You could walk everywhere, and we were allowed to do so. We'd walk to the Illinois state museum, with its dioramas (I've always like dioramas and models. Probably why I have a model train in my garage).

Springfield was one of two big stops, the other being Worcester, Mass., at which we stayed for considerable time and which were really the raison d'etre for these trips. Here we were guaranteed a) to stay with relatives, and be fawned over by aunts, uncles and grandparents, b) to play with cousins and/or local kids, and c) have some kind of lake experience which involved fishing.

My grandfather, Lou McFadden, lived at 411 S. State Street, one of those addresses that just stays with you, rolls off your tongue 50 years later. The place was magic. Built sometime in the 19th century, it had tall ceilings, doors with transoms, and one bathroom, a walk-through affair between two bedrooms, with a clawfoot tub. No shower. My grandfather, whom we called PaMac (short for GrandPaMac) eventually put a shower in the basement; it was just a showerhead that drained onto the concrete basement floor and was embarrassingly visible from the high basement windows.

The basement! I spent as much time as I could down there. It fascinated me; we didn't have basements in California. And my grandfather had lived there a long time, at least since the 1940s; it was the house in which my mom grew up. Filled with old treasures, that basement had a musty smell, dank and interesting, and to this day any musty smell reminds me of it. There were tons of tools down there; PaMac was very handy. Whenever he came to visit us in California, he fixed everything in the house that needed fixing. My dad says he was in awe of PaMac, and everything he knew, and could do. At 411, PaMac built the back porch, which held the stairs that led to the basement. In that basement was sporting equipment from early in the century, bamboo fishing poles and tackle, old bikes, including a double bike, a tall unicycle and a big-wheel bicycle my uncles would ride in local parades. Railroad lanterns – some of our relatives were railroad men in Illinois. I've loved railroads since I was a kid (yes, I'm one of those guys with a model railroad in the garage, though I don't wear overalls and a conductor's cap when I'm out there), and I have two railroad lanterns from PaMac's basement.

PaMac, in his High Point College playing days. Game face on.

He also had a shooting range down there! Well, sort of. From the front of the basement you could fire a BB gun at targets fixed to the back wall, where the dirt floor of its unfinished back rose up to meet the basement wall. So he taught us to shoot. "Squeeze the trigger like you're squeezing a lemon,", he told us.

PaMac, being a great athlete in his day, also taught us boys – and Katie - how to throw a curveball. He had played baseball and football at High Point College in North Carolina, and he had competed against Ronald "Dutch" Reagan, when he returned to finish his teaching credential at Illinois State Normal University. I have two of PaMac's baseball bats from the 1930s (my cousin Brian McFadden has his baseball gloves). The bats are long and heavy, from an era which did not value bat speed as much as it did big lumber. One is a Louisville Slugger, a Paul Waner model. Waner, nicknamed "Big Poison", played for the Pittsburgh Pirates and other clubs in the 20's and 30's. The other bat is unusual. It's a Burke Batrite, complete with bat logo (that is, the flying mammal bat), made in Athens, Georgia. Rogers Hornsby model; he played from 1915-1937. The knob end of the bat is stamped with its manufacturing date: July 15th, 1930.

PaMac explaining the curveball grip to Katie. Or maybe the spitter.

PaMac always had a twinkle in his eye, and Dan remembers his handshake: long and hard while he looked you right in the eye, almost testing you. I always thought of PaMac as a big guy. After he passed away, my Uncle Joe gave me a tweed coat that had been PaMac's, and it was really too small for me. Which surprised me. Always pictured him as bigger. But PaMac's draft registration card from 1940, when he was 34, lists him as 5'9" and 154 pounds. I'm built like him, more like a McFadden/O'Connor than a Coonan. I am wiry, at best, and probably have my mom's delicate bone structure. Dammit. Probably a big reason I "retired" from high school football after two years. On the other hand, genetics being what it is, I also received the

O'Connor hair, which turns white as you get older. But at least it's there. My brothers have Coonan hair. Which disappears.

Grandma Mac, or MaMac, was Alice O'Connor, a small, tough Irish mom (which may be redundant) of whom I have few memories; she suffered a stroke in the 1960s and passed away in 1970. My memories are of her in a wheelchair, both legs thin and encased in braces. My mom was the oldest of four. By the time we were making our cross-country auto trips, in 1967, Jim was gone; he had been killed in an auto accident, along with three other young men, in 1965. He was a motorhead and loved cars. I have vague memories of him from a train trip we took to Springfield in 1963. All the pictures from that trip show Jim and Joe in jeans and white t-shirts, prototypical early 60s youths. I remember that Jim and Joe took Terry and me out for a drive, even went to a drive-in burger place and got milkshakes. Which I'm pretty sure we spilled in the car. Those memories are a haze; Terry and I were four, about the first age at which memories stick. All I know is that Jim was gone by the time we visited in 1967. I can't imagine what it was like for my grandparents to lose a son like that. Because of Jim's death and MaMac's illness, Mom and Carol used to say that at least they had had a happy childhood.

There is a quality of toughness here, or resignation, or acceptance of suffering. Maybe that's not peculiar to the Irish, or to Irish moms, who have long known this suffering. In the 1800s and early 1900s Irish moms watched their children leave for America, many never to return. This was such a significant parting that a wake would be held for the departing son or daughter. Can't imagine. Suffering, of course, figures strongly in Catholicism (and also in Buddhism), and is offset, and surpassed, by joy. Crucifixion and resurrection. I find this quality in the McFaddens. PaMac lived another 14 years after MaMac passed. My brother Terry visited PaMac in 1984 when he was dying of

ALS, the same ailment that took another great athlete named Lou, Gehrig. PaMac said to Terry, "You know, Terry, you keep playing until you hear the whistle blow." That whistle blew for him in September of that year; he had been too sick to make it to my wedding in Santa Fe in July.

Left, PaMac and MaMac in front of 411; right, Jim, Carol, MaMac, Joe, Mom and PaMac in 1963.

So for two of those trips, PaMac and Carol were in the house at 411, and that's how I remember it. We boys would sleep on the back porch, a closed-in but not really finished space that held some chairs and extra beds and sofas, and things that did not fit in the basement or hadn't yet made it down there. Screened windows through which I'd somewhat fearfully watch summer thunderstorms (unknown in southern California). There was a record player and old 78 rpm records, such as Arthur Godfrey's non-PC Too Fat Polka ("She's too fat, she's too fat, she's too fat for me").

Mom, PaMac and Carol at the nexus - the kitchen table at 411.

My grandfather, like many older people, would be up early, in the kitchen, making coffee and listening to the farm report on the radio. Later in the day the radio broadcast would give way to a baseball game on the kitchen TV. Springfield being more in the southern part of the state than the northern, PaMac was a St. Louis Cardinals fan, rather than a Cubs fans. The huge table in the kitchen, which now resides in my parents' home in El Segundo, was from the ancestral McFadden home in Bloomington, and was the gathering point at 411. When we boys wandered in from the back porch in the morning PaMac would be drinking coffee at the table and reading the morning paper, maybe smoking his pipe. "Would you like a highball?" he'd ask us. That was code for orange juice, and we got a huge kick out of it. PaMac would sometimes fix us pancakes; he had become a good cook in his bachelorhood. He'd break off the uneven edge of the pancake, the little plop of almost sliver-dollar-sized cooked batter, and say to us, "Here's your allowance." When I was at Notre Dame, Terry and I, and then Dan, would take the train down from South Bend to Springfield for Thanksgiving at PaMac's.

PaMac spent his career in education. He taught PE, I believe, at the high school level, and then spent 20-plus years as principal at Metheny Elementary School. He was involved in teachers unions, serving for a while as president of the Illinois State Federation of Teachers. Both of my parents were children during World War II, and the stories of the sacrifices made on behalf of the war effort resonated with me. Apparently very few drove cars during the war, maybe because of lack of gasoline and rubber for tires. GrandPaMac put his car up on blocks (in the garage he had built) for the duration of the war, and walked everywhere. Everyone did. Mom and her siblings walked to St. Agnes School. Certain foods were in short supply, and were rationed, allocated via ration stamps. Butter was scant, and so folks ate oleo (margarine) instead. PaMac, like others, planted a Victory Garden. Again, that resilience, that grit.

When we arrived in Springfield, we pulled into the alley behind 411 and parked in front of the garage, which was a one-horse barn until PaMac got after it. PaMac's neighbor, Don Jeffers, told us he'd always say, "The gypsies are here!" when our car pulled in. All this was a wonder to me. An alley – we didn't have those in my neighborhood in El Segundo. I can still hear the sound the tires made when they left the brick street and rolled over the gravel of the alley. And there was no fence separating PaMac's yard from the alley (there is now, 50 years later) nor were there fences between some of the yards. How could that work? How did dogs stay in the yards? They didn't one time I was riding on of PaMc's ancient bikes and a dog lit out from a yard and chased me down the street. And coming from southern California's dry Mediterranean climate, I couldn't help but notice how lush the neighborhood was. Stuff just grew there. Big old Midwestern broadleaf trees, maples and oaks, which didn't so much border yards as just blur the property lines, with their generous overhang. That is frowned upon in southern California. I've had neighbors trim my overhanging trees and throw the trimmings over the fence into my yard.

Left, The Coonan-McFadden band packs them in at 411. Right, the Jeffers boys: Steve, Pete and Mike.

But the alley. We'd hang out there, playing ditch with my cousins and with the neighbor kids, the Jeffers. Because we could! Even after dinner! It was warm out, and the light lasted a long time in the summer. And then the fireflies came out, and that was a trip. What the fuck? We did not have little glowing bugs in SoCal. In later years my kids, too would love the fireflies, at Cathy's parent's home on Delevan Lake, Wisconsin.

Cousins were automatic playmates, like siblings you just didn't happen to live with. Brian, Kevin and Mike McFadden belonged to Uncle Joe, who was then married to Marilyn Vespa. The Vespa family had a place on Lake Springfield, and we spent time with the cousins out there, swimming and fishing. PaMac, who was a hunter and a fisherman, had huge bamboo poles in his basement, and with these we went after the catfish that lived in Lake Springfield. GrandPaMac, in shirtsleeves (he, and my dad, were from generations which didn't wear shorts. Whereas I hate pants and wear shorts every day) and with his ever-present pipe, would patiently bait our poles and teach us to fish, even watching the poles, when our patience timed out, one foot on a pole. That's how I caught a fish there. PaMac caught it for me, while I had stepped away. That catfish was taken back to 411 and fried up, and it was pretty exciting for me. I am not really an angler but I have been fishing a few times, and I can tell you every fish I've caught. There have been that few of them. I caught a small bass at Lake Almanor when I was a kid, and I caught a tuna on the one ocean fishing trip I've been on. And that may be it. In the same vein, I can tell you every important or notable play I've made in sports; there have been that few of them, as well. In Little League, as an otherwise light-hitting second baseman, I hit a double off the wall for the major league Tigers to tie the league championship game. Which we went on to win, entitling us to get our butts kicked by the Giants from the other side of town; they had Bob Helsom, a future major league prospect, who actually threw curveballs as a 12-year old. They were the first curves I had ever seen, and had me bailing out of the batter's box. We really stood no chance.

We and the cousins loved to hang out in PaMac's unfinished back porch. There were some old musical instruments out there, and we took them up, temporarily forming the Coonan-McFadden Band, which was more like a concept, than an actual band. Much like Steely Dan. Heavy on rhythm, we were, and light on melody. Or vocals. Nonetheless we made the adults listen to our atonal music, and they recorded the moment. There has been no mention of a reunion tour.

Occasionally we hung out with Joe and Anne Ineich. Right, the whole gang at 411 in 1976.

The other kids we played with were the Jeffers, who lived next door to GrandPaMac. I think they were a little bit wilder than we were. Mike was closest to our age, maybe a year older than Terry and me, and we did typical kid stuff. Rode bikes, played catch, played ditch. But one year we went back, and Mike had changed. He was a surly teenager, and was actually mean, and to me, a lightweight, a little threatening. Huge lesson. People change, and sometimes not for the better. Another lesson: teenager is a rough occupation.

I was beginning to feel my oats, as a teenager. The oldest Jeffers, Terry, had a great record collection, including that wonderful Herb Alpert album, with the woman covered in whipped cream. Left quite an impression on me. As did Katy Jeffers, the cute younger sister of Mike. I definitely was beginning to take notice of the fairer sex, particularly on our 1976 trip, between my junior and senior years in high school. On that trip we spent significant time with the Ineich kids, Joe and Anne, who lived in Jacksonville. Their dad, Paul, was my dad's roommate at Notre Dame, and their mom, Sallie, was Mom's best friend; they had arranged the blind date that led eventually to my parents' 60-plus years of wedded bliss! In fact, Springfield was where my mom and dad were married, in 1957, after countless nights in the couch at 411 when Dad visited Mom there, coming down from Notre Dame. Personally, I found Anne Ineich to be pretty cute. And those kids were runners, like me; Joe would end up at Notre Dame with myself and Terry. Never saw Anne Ineich again. Or Katy Jeffers.

In 1957, Mom and Dad married at St. Agnes Church in Springfield. Aunt Carol was maid of honor, though her shoes stayed on at the reception (more on that later).

With my long, oily, 1970s hair and aviator-style glasses, I had no idea of what was up or down in the world of relationships. But I sure began to recognize what I liked. Aunt Sheila, for one. By 1976 Uncle Joe was married to Sheila: sharp features, sharp tongue, dark skin (there that is again). I was hooked. Like facing Bob Helsom, I stood no chance. One time I was sitting with everyone else at the crowded table in PaMac's kitchen. Sheila maneuvered around the end of the table, putting her hands on my shoulders as she squeezed past. A charge of electricity coursed through me. Oh, seventeen.

We also toured the sites in Springfield and surrounds, relatives in tow. We became steeped in Lincoln lore, visiting his house, law offices, former home in New Salem, and his tomb at Oak Ridge Cemetery. So weird to think of the great man, entombed in there, after a long solemn, slow train ride brought his remains back to Springfield from Washington. How could such a great man, whose work was not quite done, be taken so suddenly and randomly from the country?

We soaked up Lincoln lore at his home and tomb.

Lincoln was so Midwestern. Salt of the earth. Solid citizen, like my McFadden cousins. Between those three McFadden boys, and us six Coonan kids, my Aunt Carol did not lack for nieces and nephews to dote on. Carol had never married, and had even planned on entering the convent for a while. The McFaddens were preparing to say goodbye to her forever; it was one of the cloistered orders, who separate themselves from society, and their families, for good. It didn't happen, and I'm not sure why. But I'm not alone in thinking it would have not been a great fit, for at least one reason: Carol was a notorious night owl and slept as late as she could. Hard to imagine her making it to morning prayers in time. Or at all. As it was, she still dedicated her life to others, as a social worker.

Carol sometimes took us kids to the Illinois state fair, which was mindblowing. State fairs are HUGE. And we had never even been to the LA County fair. I still remember the midway there, with its freak shows: bearded women, midgets, strongmen. I had no idea. Kind of a little scary. But there was Carol, laughing away the whole time, in her white summer pants and striped top. Life was good when you were with Carol.

Beloved and inimitable Aunt Carol, "AC", willing foil for her goddamn nephews.

Carol was the happiest person many of us will ever know. She could not go more than 10 seconds without laughing. She just got a kick out of everything, and she had such a special relationship with her nieces and nephews. She called Katie and Nora her "sweet nieces", whereas we boys were her "dadgum nephews". Which Dan later changed to "goddamn nephews" and that stuck. Carol was too prim to say that, of course (unlike our generation) and so in correspondence she would refer to her "g.d." nephews. And we dogged her mercilessly. Dan would hoist her up, on many occasions, and she would just laugh. We began a tradition of drinking out her of shoe at family weddings. It got to the point where she would hide in the bathroom at wedding receptions to avoid anyone taking her shoe. Dan gave her eulogy, and drank out of her shoe at that event, too; Carol couldn't avoid the shoe-drinking, even in death.

For as much as we hung out with other kids in Springfield, and toured the sites with family, I didn't mind, at all, spending time by myself at 411. I could while away hours poking through the basement. There was an attic, too; though we didn't go up there; it was accessed by a pull-down ladder from a trap-door in the ceiling – the very high ceiling – above the kitchen. I maybe went up there once. After PaMac had passed, Uncle Joe found a brace of Civil War pistols up in that attic.

I also spent considerable time in the library, the hallway leading from the front door to the living room. PaMac had built floor-to-ceiling shelves in that hallway, and they were packed with books by the time we made our visits. Among the treasures were some law books that had belonged to Lincoln! They came from the personal library of a Judge David Davis, who had lived in Bloomington, and had been an associate of Lincoln's, even serving as his campaign manager and in his cabinet. One of PaMac's relatives, Minnie O'Toole (I know, that sounds like it was made up) was the caretaker for the Judge Davis house, and PaMac ended up with the books. Form your own conclusions. For all I know, Minnie may have made off with the Judge's silver, as well. And those Civil War pistols…maybe Minnie O'Toole's fingerprints are on them still.

One of the books in the hall absolutely captivated me. Mystery at Laughing Water was a book my mom had read as a child, about a Nancy Drew-type teen who solves a mystery while at summer camp in the North Woods. Maybe it was the natural setting, or the mythos surrounding a summer camp to which everyone returns. Coulda been the kid-solving-a-mystery thing.

Encyclopedia Brown, the Hardy Boys, Jupiter Jones and the Three Investigators, The Mad Scientists Club...I was a sucker for all of that. Ate it up. At age 10, I wanted to be a detective when I grew up, and I started a (short-lived) detective agency. I booked one case, which was never solved. I suppose that makes it a cold case, and maybe I should circle back around to solving it. Pick up the trail. Other career ambitions were equally unreachable: when I was in sixth grade, I wanted to be an NFL wide receiver, like my hero Jack Snow of the Rams. Delusions of grandeur. But in fourth grade, I wanted to be a forest ranger. Wrote an essay about it, illustrated it with a drawing of me standing on the deck of a fire lookout tower, peering through binoculars. And wearing a flat hat. A Ranger hat. Exactly like the one I wore (or avoided wearing) for the National Park Service. Seeds sown in fourth grade, and maybe on those cross-country trips.

Anyway, I liked Mystery at Laughing Water so much that later in life I bought of copy for my girls, when they were old enough to read it. They never took to it, like some other things I tried to interest them in: The Hobbit/Lord of the Rings. Catholicism. But, like those things, it's there if they ever want to pick it up.

Springfield has always been a place charged with emotion and memory for me. Why is that? Because of GrandPaMac, the second finest man I've ever known (my dad is first)? Because of the grit and resilience, the persistence, of that McFadden family, weathering wars and untimely loss of family members, and illness? I've long believed that persistence is the only quality that really matters. Was it because of the primacy of family? There's also that sense of place...kindly, stately 411 was the center of the McFadden world for 50-plus years, and had an aura of history itself. The basement packed with vintage. Tall ceilings and transoms. The front hallway bookcase with books that belonged to Lincoln. Clawfoot tub in the bathroom. A brace of Civil War pistols in the attic.

411 was also a window into the Midwest for me, a portal into a world very unlike where I grew up, and one in which I would spend – gladly – my college years. Flat, fertile land, rivers and streams clogged with trees and foliage, leaves turning in the fall. A sense of belonging. I didn't stay in the Midwest to live, but the Midwest stayed in me.

When Cathy and the kids and I drove through Springfield one year, we pulled into that alley behind 411. My grandfather was long gone, and someone else lived there. Cathy was driving. I rolled down the window and took it all in and the memories came rushing back. I missed my grandfather, and our time at 411. I cried like a baby as we drove away, down the alley.

Bricks and Ivy

As we left Springfield, we headed north, past other cities, such as Decatur and Bloomington, that had figured prominently in McFadden and O'Connor history. PaMac was born in Decatur; both he and Mom received their teaching credentials in Normal-Bloomington, at what was then Illinois State Normal University. Come to think of it, there has been an inordinate number of teachers in my family. Six of the eight of us Coonans have taught at some level.

One might think we were heading toward Chicago, that city of the big shoulders, and Wrigley Field and Ernie Banks, Michigan Avenue, Gino's East and Pizzeria Uno, but we in fact skirted Chicago every time. We were headed to the east coast, a two-day drive by the 8-hour/500-mile formula, and Chicago just wasn't a good stopping point for us. Later, I would spend considerable time there, even got married there once. Cathy was from Downer's Gove, a northwestern suburb, and we visited there with the girls quite often. But in 1967 now we had bigger quarry, the East Coast, and our route east toward Massachusetts would take us along I80, below Lakes Michigan and Erie, and not coincidently, through South Bend, Indiana. Surely you've heard of the place? Where French traders settled on the south bend of the St. Joseph River in the 1820s? Ah, you say, there's another reason…it's the home of Notre Dame. A place, arguably, that trumps Howard Johnson's as the most significant stop on our treks, due to its place in our family history, and its influence on our family, to this day. So settle in, because we're going to spend a little time here at Notre Dame.

Three future ND grads in 1967, left, and a view of the Golden Dame on our visit in 1976, when we stayed overnight – in a dorm.

What are we, if not a Notre Dame family? My dad and my uncle went there, as did Terry, Dan and myself. My sister Katie married a Notre Dame guy (Jim), and their daughter Colleen went there. We grew up Notre Dame fans in the LA area, home of archrival USC, and that has to be the definition of a siege mentality. Notre Dame: where my dad met my mom, and proposed to her. We have arranged family weddings around Notre Dame football games: in 1988 Kate and Jim were married the day after Thanksgiving and a day before the Notre Dame-USC football game. The Irish beat the Trojans 27-10 and went on to win the national championship. That turned out to be one of the greatest years in family history. Because the Dodgers won the World Series that year, too. The Notre Dame fight song, the Victory March, has been played at weddings and funerals.

All through my youth, I never really wanted to go to any college but Notre Dame. Growing up, Terry and I had ND gear – including football helmets! – from early on. As a kid, I'd pour over my dad's Notre Dame yearbooks, with their black and white photos of the campus and the mostly white, all-male students dressed sensibly, as they did in the 50s: slacks, leather shoes, v-neck sweaters, having a mostly male collegiate good time, at least the kind of good time that makes the yearbook. Of course, in California, we were a long way from Notre Dame, and perhaps that made it even more exotic and desirable. A Catholic Camelot.

Every other year, the Notre Dame football team would travel west to play USC (or Southern Cal, as they were known then) around Thanksgiving time. It was - and is – the greatest intersectional rivalry in college football; Notre Dame has played USC annually since the days of Knute Rockne. And my parents would go to the games, in the LA Coliseum. Including the 1966 shellacking of USC by Notre Dame, a 51-0 embarrassment of the Trojans on their own turf. But the next time they came out, in 1968, Mom didn't go; Dad still had the extra ticket, and he flipped a coin to see whether Terry or I would accompany him. Terry won, and he and Dad watched the Irish tie the undefeated and number one Trojans, 21-21. I did get to go to the communion breakfast, the day following the game. These were events put on by the Notre Dame Club of Los Angeles, at which the team would have breakfast and celebrate Mass in a hotel ballroom, with a player at each table sharing it with local ND grads and their families. For us, this was a brush with greatness, even better than being at the game. There was a Notre Dame football player sitting at our table! At the end, we could go around the room and get autographs on our football programs. I still have mine, pasted into a scrapbook I put together about Notre Dame football. Joe Theismann's autograph! I had other favorites, like Reggie Barnett, cornerback; I chose his number, 14, for freshman football in high school.

One year we sat with safety John Dubenetsky, who told an off-color story about a nun recognizing him walking around naked in a dorm. Hunh? College is like that? He also had huge hands; he passed the water pitcher around with one hand, just engulfing it. Of course, the really lucky families sat with the stars of the team. The way it worked, each player was seated at a table when the doors opened for families. There was a mad rush by kids to tables with the stars. It was pandemonium and chaos. You know, Oklahoma land rush-type stuff. My brother Dan was closing in on a star's table one year, and knocked over a tray of orange juices along the way. We did not tell my mother about that. We were denied a star that year, anyway; a prominent ND grad in the LA area was already sitting at that table. Privilege.

Notre Dame got their butt kicked regularly by USC back in the early 1970s. We would sit in the stands, often in the pouring rain, among drunk Trojan fans, watching the Irish fail. One year, 1974, Notre Dame had a 24-6 halftime lead only to lose 55-24 on the strength of Trojan Anthony Davis' four touchdowns. In the rain. I remember the rain soaking my jeans as I sat on the old wooden benches in the Coliseum endzone, watching the horror unfold with my dad and brothers. I would not see Notre Dame beat USC until I went to college.

The Coliseum was home to the 1932, and later the 1984, Olympics, and is old and cavernous. As part of the relatively few Notre Dame faithful we took considerable abuse from the USC fans, even though we were kids. We grew to despise USC and its cardinal-and-gold colors, its white horse and ersatz Trojan garb, and it's incessant, irritating playing of its fight song. But that is also the cherished Notre Dame football experience I grew up with. Notre Dame in its white away jerseys entering the lion's den, to wage righteous war in enemy territory. The sight of the Notre Dame team, in their white jerseys, amassed in the tunnel of the Coliseum, moved me; my team, my people, were here. The sight moves me to this day, and I prefer seeing Notre Dane in their away whites. And the smell of cigar smoke will always take me back to the Coliseum bathrooms, with dozens of cigar-smoking, raucous, older USC fans in red jackets whooping it up as they crowded toward the long, common urinal (also a formative experience for me!). Make way for that little Notre Dame kid.

In later years my spite turned to grudging respect for USC and its storied rivalry with the Irish. My family now counts some rabid Trojan fans among its closest friends. And I no longer live and die according to the Saturday fortunes of the Irish. Notre Dame football losses used to ruin my weekends, but I've long out grown that. Still pisses me off, of course.

Thus when I was a kid my only contact with Notre Dame were these every-other-year football games out in LA. But on our 1967 trip we stopped by campus, and in 1976, before our senior year in high school, we not only stopped by campus, but we stayed overnight there. By that time Notre Dame was opening up some dorms for family summer visits, and we stayed in Lewis Hall, behind the Dome. Terry and I even had interviews at the admissions office, though I doubt they had much impact on the admission process. In those days, before Notre Dame became the super elite school it is today, being a "legacy" really counted, as Notre Dame valued the "Notre Dame family" concept. And my SAT scores were pretty decent, but they wouldn't get me into ND these days.

My dad started this whole Notre Dame thing. Changed the arc of this family forever, even began the whole family trajectory. How did he end up there? He grew up in Annapolis, where his

dad, my grandfather, was a metallurgy professor at the Naval
Academy. Catholic, of course, and so Dad attended St. Mary's
High School. Like Terry, he was a guard on the football team
(and he was senior class president, like Terry), and also played
lacrosse, which was an exotic Eastern sport I associated only
with the Iroquois. Dad had – and still has – his lacrosse sticks
from high school, beautiful curved wooden sticks, now deeply
colored from weathering and sweat, still with some of the leather
webbing intact. Dad says that when he was a high school senior,
he decided he wanted a college that was Catholic, and offered
chemical engineering. In addition to Notre Dame, he had also
applied to Holy Cross, in Worcester, and St. Mary's, in Moraga,
California, but found both unimpressive. So he accepted the
offer from Notre Dame, without ever having visited the campus.

**Tom and Kay on their momentous first date, left, and in 1991 at the
Grotto, where she had said "yes" 35 years before.**

And that, his decision to go to ND, changed the world
forever, akin to Columbus stumbling upon the New World or
the Wright Brothers fooling around with airfoils. Upon such
small and sometimes random events are built the foundations of
new worlds. The butterfly effect. If Dad had gone to Holy Cross,
what then? No West Coast Coonans, that's for sure. Dad's good

friend and ND roommate was the aforementioned Paul Ineich, whose hometown honey, Sally Costa, was Mom's best friend. Sal and Paul arranged for some Springfield gals to travel to Notre Dame for blind dates on the weekend of the Notre Dame – Southern Cal game in 1954. Here's where chance, or fate, came into play again. Evidently Paul had lined up 10 guys, but Sal had lined up only 8 gals. The guys drew straws. What if my dad had drawn the short straw? When the group first met, the morning of the football game (the girls had stayed in the South Bend YWCA), Dad signaled to Paul that he wanted to be paired with THAT one – Mom. The rest, as they say, is history. In 1956 Dad asked Mom to marry him at the Grotto, spiritual center of Notre Dame, and she said yes. It was a foregone conclusion – they had known they were heading that way for months. Apparently, they were serious after only a couple of dates. Still, they called Kay's family to tell them of the decision. PaMac said they'd vote on it. The outcome was favorable, though it may not have been unanimous; in fact, it very well could have been a 3-2 split decision. Turned out to stand the test of time, a blessed union that lasted almost 63 years. I used to joke that I also proposed marriage at the Grotto, numerous times, but no one took me up on it.

If you don't know, Notre Dame has a dome, the Golden Dome, on its administrative building, and northern Indiana being pretty much as flat as Illinois, that dome can be seen for miles. It's certainly visible from I80, which passes just north of the campus, and on flights to and from South Bend. I can only imagine how far it could be seen back in the day (it was built in 1878) though no doubt more of the surrounding area was wooded then. It is one of several campus features that are storied and iconic, and impressive to 8-year old rabid Notre Dame fans. Other sites are the Grotto, a replica of the grotto at

Lourdes, France, where Mary appeared to St. Bernadette, and the Log Cabin, site of the first building at Notre Dame, erected by Fr. Sorin one snowy winter in 1842.

Yes, it's actually gilded with gold leaf.

We took it all in on our 1967 trip. But also…Notre Dame Stadium! The House that Rockne built! Literally. He was the architect. The field where Notre Dame football teams had played since 1930. We HAD to peek in there. Football stadiums, like baseball parks, are a little eerie in the off-season, with no screaming fans, no uniform-clad players on the field, no tailgating. But they're also a little…reverential. They're huge and quiet, but you KNOW momentous things, of quasi-religious importance, maybe even matters of near-life or death, have occurred there in the past and will again in the future. They're kinda like cathedrals, really. We took it all in, the field where Rockne and Leahy coached and the Four Horsemen played. No doubt we dreamed of not only attending games there, but playing them for the Fighting Irish. Hey, a boy can dream, can't he? Then we probably went to the bookstore and bought Notre Dame gear.

Left, Notre Dame Stadium on a quiet summer day in 1976. Right, Coonans made it back to the stadium many times when it was not so quiet, or warm.

Dad's experience at Notre Dame was everything he had wanted it to be, and more. He had not seen many college campuses prior to arriving at Notre Dame, and he says he was awed by it all, the beautiful lake setting in particular.

It was Catholic for sure. In Dad's day, students, all of them male, were required to attend Mass in the dorm chapel three times a week, though apparently you could check in (a ND football player had the job of checking your name against the hall roster) and then go back to bed. PE was required for freshman, and still was, when I was there, and part of the PE rotation was swimming; you had to pass a swim test before taking other PE classes. In my day, as in my Dad's, this was done at "The Rock", the large gym and swimming pool at the end of South Quad. When Dad arrived poolside for his swim test, he was the only one wearing trunks. None of the other guys were wearing anything. Yeah. Well. The lack of women on campus was so taken for granted that one time, in a chemistry class of over 100, Dad heard a woman's voice and turned around; a nun was auditing the class.

Dad's studies were successful. When he arrived at ND, he was torn between studying chemical engineering, or metallurgy, like his dad. His advisor, Dr. Rich, told him he didn't have to make a decision yet, since the classes would be the same for several years. Dad liked chemical engineering so well that he stayed on an extra year at Notre Dame to receive his master's in it.

I assume Dad hit the books pretty hard. The second half of freshman year included physics, and there was a test every other Tuesday night, which caused absolute panic among the students the weekend before. On the first such test, Dad received 100, and was so proud that he sent the test to his dad. However, he couldn't keep that pace up! To clear his head after these Tuesday physics exams, Dad would walk around the Notre Dame lakes, alone. I, too, loved the lakes, which were part of my regular running route at ND. And I took freshman chem from the same professor, Emil T. Hofman, that had taught freshmen chem in my dad's day (then as a graduate assistant). His weekly quizzes were brutal, and I have no doubt my dad did much better than I on them.

In Dad's day, there were even classes on Saturday mornings, in fact, four of them. Except on football Saturdays, when one class was dropped so students could go to the games. This contrasted with my Notre Dame football Saturday mornings. The only studying we did was how to tap the keg for the tailgater.

Socially, Dad made friends for life at Notre Dame, as we all do in college. Notre Dame students hailed from all parts of the country, and ended up all over after graduation. Dad's good buddies were Paul Ineich from Illinois, Frank Conte from Pittsburgh (Frank and Paul, the heroes from Dad's stories), and Fred Brinskelli from North Carolina. In Dad's day, dorms were arranged by class: there were four freshman dorms, four sophomore dorms, etc. And the freshman dorms were furthest from the dining hall! Dad's freshman dorm was Breen-Phillips (BP), and the first floor housed Notre Dame's athletic department; coaches and athletes filed through on a daily basis. The second floor of BP housed many chemical engineering students, including Frank and Fred, but Dad was on the more diverse fourth floor with his roommate Kenny Davis, also from St. Mary's High School in Annapolis. Paul, a preprofessional major who went on to dental school, was several doors down from Dad.

In those days, the electricity went off on the dorm floors at 11 p.m., to ensure, literally, lights out. The only lights that remained on were those in the bathrooms, and guys could be found studying late at night in there. Dad and his buddies occasionally ventured into the attic and out onto the roof of BP, and Dad carved his initials in a staircase on the fourth floor of the dorm. I found those initials, years later.

Dad and Frank had PE together and took boxing for one of the quarterly assignments. Frank outweighed Dad by 100 pounds, and both were surprised when Dad hauled off and landed a big punch. In fact, Dad was a good boxer, having trained in high school under the Navy boxing coach, Spike Webb, when Pop was teaching at the Naval Academy.

Night life? When asked what he did on weekends, Dad told me that he studied a lot. Uh, yeah...we did, too. In Dad's day Washington Hall, on campus, showed two movies a day, and the guys would also occasionally walk into South Bend for dinner and a movie. Women from St. Mary's, the college across the street, would come over on buses for dances held every Saturday night at the Fieldhouse, which otherwise housed the university's basketball court and an indoor dirt track. During football season they called these "Victory Dances" whether Notre Dame had won or not. And during Dad's time ND had losing seasons, despite having Heisman winner and future Green Bay Packer Paul Hornung. Hornung was a notorious partying rascal during his Packer years, and I assume he did not spend his Notre Dame weekends "studying a lot".

Left, graduation day at Notre Dame in 1956: Ted, Pat, Pop, Nana and Dad, in his Army ROTC uniform. Right, my parents visited campus 60 years later, for his 60-year reunion.

For some years after graduation, Dad, Frank, Paul and Fred met annually at a Notre Dame football game. During the campus visits they often looked up one of their old chemical engineering professors, Dr. Kohn, who was happy to see them. Dad reports that before his classes, while waiting for Dr. Kohn to arrive, the guys would pitch pennies against the wall. Dr. Kohn was single and was very socially "active". He took his chemical engineering students into Chicago to tour refineries, but Dr.

Kohn himself would skip the tour and instead make time with the office secretary.

Dad and Mom maintained regular correspondence with his buddies and their wives all their lives; I remember seeing Sallie Ineich's distinctive handwriting on Christmas cards and letters every year. In later years Mom and Dad attended Notre Dame reunions and thoroughly enjoyed seeing their lifelong friends. I accompanied my parents to the ND reunion in 2016; my class ('81) and his ('56) were on the same five-year reunion cycle. At the end of the weekend, as I drove them away from campus, my dad asked me to drive up Notre Dame Avenue, the entrance to campus, for a final view of the Golden Dome. He was misty-eyed as we did this. He told me he thought it would be his last time seeing the campus, and his friends. How important was this place to him, and to us? Probably no place, outside of El Segundo, holds more weight for us, more gravitas, than does Notre Dame.

I was enamored of the place from early on, beginning, as I mentioned, with my dad's yearbooks. To me, Notre Dame in those black-and-white yearbook pictures just looked like what a college was supposed to look like: grassy quads, bricks and ivy, big trees (none of them palm trees!). And it had a history, an aura about it. Notre Dame seemed to be ABOUT something, something bigger than just college. I would find that to be true, though perhaps not in the obvious, Catholic way. And it was shrouded in myth. Larger-than-life characters...Fr. Sorin, Rockne, George Gipp, The Four Horsemen, Ted Hesburgh. Both the university itself, and its football program, had what you might call creation myths, or at least characters and plot that lend themselves to creation mythmaking. Fr. Sorin, after having convinced his superiors in France that he could and should establish a college in northern Indiana, hewed his

way through the northern Indiana wilderness and founded
Notre Dame in a log cabin by a snowy lake in 1842. Un-hunh.
Knute Rockne, a chemistry grad student at Notre Dame, took
a somewhat established but local college football program,
invented the forward pass, and put that team on the train and
barn-stormed across the country, holding their own against the
powerful service academies and Southern Cal. Rockne's Raiders,
the Fighting Irish, become a college football powerhouse and
one of the premiere sporting attractions of the 1920's, right up
there with the Ruth and Gehrig Yankees. Heck, Notre Dame
even played to a full house in Yankee Stadium. A dying George
Gipp asking Rockne, on his death bed, to have the boys win one
for the Gipper someday, which they did. A relatively unknown
Notre Dame backfield being immortalized by Grantland Rice as
the Four Horsemen of the Apocalypse ("Outlined against a blue-
gray October sky…"). The stuff of legend! The beloved coach
Rockne dying in a plane crash in a Kansas cornfield. I mean,
you can't make this stuff up. It's no wonder they made a movie
about it. By the way, that movie, Knute Rockne, All-American,
was filmed at Notre Dame in the late 1930s and has wonderful
footage of campus. I ate all of this up.

Carroll Hall? Where is That?

Left, heading off to ND, August 1977, baseball bat in hand. Right, Carroll Hall sits in splendid isolation on the far side of St. Mary's Lake.

When Terry and I were accepted for admittance to ND in 1977, it had to be a great moment for my dad, a chance for us, the next generation, to be part of this continuum, this arc which he and Mom had started, part of our family's own creation myth, as it were. But we were not pressured to go there, at all. I had also applied to Santa Clara University, and UC Davis, which had a strong science program that attracted me. I'm sure the acceptance letter from ND arrived sometime in the early spring, but I know Terry and I didn't say yes to ND until late in the spring. Perhaps I was dithering, weighing that strong UC Davis science program against Notre Dame. In any case, our late acceptance of Notre Dame's invitation had one cataclysmic consequence: we were low on the list for choice of dorm. Now,

Dad knew all the ND dorms, had lived in four of them, and so we had good advice and had made thoughtful, deliberate decisions about our choices. None of which we got! A letter arrived from ND saying we had been placed in Carroll Hall, a dorm my dad had never heard of! We had to get out a campus map to find it. And it was BARELY on the campus map.

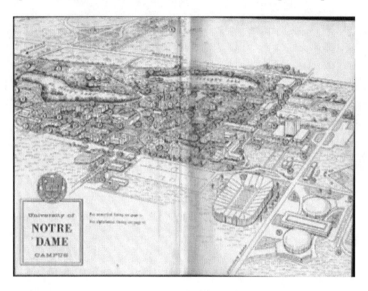

A 1969 campus map shows Carroll Hall, labeled number 1 on the map (and in my heart), practically off the map on the far western end of campus.

Carroll Hall! Our assignment there was another crazy turn of evolution. Had we been assigned to one of the more traditional, and normal, dorms, our Notre Dame experience might have been more...normal. It was anything but at Carroll Hall. The reason my dad hadn't heard of it as an undergrad hall was because it hadn't been one, until the year Terry and I were accepted to ND. Carroll had been a graduate student residence for some years, and before that had been a formation house for brothers of the Holy Cross order. Isolation is a critical component of formation, and the brothers housed at Carroll had it in spades. Carroll sits in splendid isolation on the far western border of campus. Only Highway 31 separates it from St. Mary's College, and it's actually closer to much of the SMC campus than to Notre Dame's, from which it is separated by St. Mary's Lake. When we finally found it on the map, we were somewhat disappointed, and apprehensive, figuring (pretty much rightly so) that our experience there would not be a typical ND one. We even talked about the possibility of transferring to another dorm in our sophomore year.

In addition to being distant from the main Notre Dame campus, Carroll Hall is…old. Built in 1906. Four stories of dorm rooms, all high ceilings and transoms above the doors (like 411 South State Street!). Steam heat gurgling through radiator pipes in the winter. No air conditioning. No established history as a Notre Dame dorm, like Corby or Dillon or Sorin. No association with a women's dorm. Not close to the cafeteria.

So, in 1977, Carroll was nobody's first choice as a dorm. It seemed as though everyone in there that first year had accepted ND's invitation late, or had been a late admittance. And it was mostly freshmen! There were 55 of us, more or less, and less than a handful were upper classmen. And they were there because they wanted the isolation (a couple of apparently gay students valued the privacy out there; this was decades before the sea-change in thinking about that). We, the freshmen, were there because we were the surfeit, the overflow. And whether it was our nature, or the isolation made us this way, we were misfits. Island of the misfit toys. And…we were in charge.

Terry and I took a red-eye flight from LA to Chicago in late August 1977, then a commuter flight to South Bend. We had requested to room together, and had been assigned to a double on Carroll's third floor. Carroll sits, somewhat majestically, on a rise beyond a long grassy lawn that slopes down to St. Mary's Lake. That lawn has been used for football, snow football, concerts, ultimate frisbee, and just plain fooling around. In recent years the university built a sand volleyball court right in front of the hall. One of the first events we freshmen took part in was a football game, with pretty much all the hall residents, on that lawn. It was a madhouse. One freshman, Mark Mocarski, dropped a pass and was generally berated for it, and claimed later that the dropped pass set the tone for his tenure at Carroll.

Spring 1979, Carroll Hall. The inmates clearly ran this asylum.

Notre Dame, and northern Indiana, was lush and humid and warm when we arrived on campus in late August. Cicadas buzzing in the deep green of the trees. We adjusted to the physical location of Carroll, even grew to love it. It was a long walk to south Dining Hall, but luckily that was on the way to class. Terry, in particular, had an affinity for the dining hall hot breakfast: institutional scrambled eggs, some kind of potatoes, trays of soggy bacon, pancakes that had sat in the warmer a long time, maybe even since the night before. We had 8 a.m. math classes all the way on the other side of campus, and it was an early start to get that hot breakfast. Terry got a job at the dining hall and became somewhat of an institution there, befriending the South Bend residents who worked there, such as beloved Bev, who just worshipped Terry. He had that effect on many older women. The priest thing.

From the upper floors of Carroll Hall, the view was...distracting.

We were the only dorm that had their own gym. An ancient brick gym stood behind Carroll. It had no insulation and the brick walls started just a foot or two beyond the endline. But it was ours, nobody else's, and available for hoops any time, night or day. Plenty of drunken, or high, late-night hoops were played out there, after studying or after the bars shut down.

And we had the lake. The two lakes were on my running route, as were the nature trails over at St. Mary's College. Running the Notre Dame lakes worked for me the way walking them did for my dad. And it was a shame to have the lake right there, and no way to enjoy it; small sailboats were available for use on the other lake, St. Joseph's, but boats were not allowed on St. Mary's. But life finds a way, as Malcom said in Jurassic Park. Chris Stoughton, one of my sophomore roommates, worked at summer camp in Ohio and brought back a canoe. I mean a full-on canoe. We stored it in the basement at Carroll and used it only at night, when ND security was less likely to see it. As it was, we ended up playing cat and mouse with ND security, who would spot the canoe and drive to the side of the lake where they thought they had seen it. By this time we were behind one of the small islands or on the other side. And that canoe was another incentive to get women out to Carroll; it was borrowed sometimes for dates.

I fell quickly in love with the whole setting. From my dorm window, I could gaze past the stately trees and over the lake to the beacon-like Dome and the spires of Sacred Heart Cathedral, the big church on campus. It was great to wake up to that view, and to come home to it. In fall the trees that framed that view, the maples, oaks and walnuts, molted to brilliant reds, yellows and oranges. I had never seen this, a real fall.

Fall also bought football season, of course. Football was such an integral part of the Notre Dame experience that I can't imagine being happy at a college that didn't have it. Following, even living, the fortunes of a top and storied program, from the hot humid days of late summer to the cold, bare days of November and into the bowl season provided a weekly focus that united everyone. We quickly took to the tailgating, of course. Tailgating! The one time it's okay to start drinking in the early morning! Start early and pace yourself, I always say. In those days students could park and tailgate on the huge green field (called, appropriately enough, Greenfield) south of the stadium. So one of the few cars at Carroll would claim a spot early. We would make it over a little later. Rumely would buy a keg and roll it from the street over to the the tailgater, if he couldn't drive in. The dorm owned a tap which would be somewhat ceremoniously attached to the keg, and that's a little harder to do than you think. There is so much potential in a freshly tapped keg. And it's what I call "goal-oriented" drinking: you gotta finish the keg (later in life I would co-own a kegerator, a small fridge that houses a keg, which meant that you actually DIDN'T have to finish the keg).

Football Saturdays were a beehive of activity on campus. Crisp fall air (eventually). Families and alums and fans walking around campus, seeing the sights before the game (the Grotto was crowded, maybe everybody proposed there), and descending on the bookstore for ND apparel. Footballs flying across the quad, and barbecues sizzling outside many of the dorms. At the tailgater we grilled brats on a small barbecue, and I will always associate brats with college football season. As the season wore on, tailgating grew colder, and I learned the concept of the drinking glove; you could share a pair of gloves with your buddy. The gloved hand held the beer, and your other hand went in your pocket.

Sometimes we stayed so late at the tailgater that we were late entering the stadium, and at one game freshman year, the Air Force game, I didn't make it into the stadium at all. At the tailgater, well after the game started, I ended up facedown in the half-frozen mud of Greenfield. After a minute Rumely looked at Hogan and said, "Do you think we should get him up?' College was such a formative experience for me.

Notre Dame won the national championship during that freshman year, making for one of the most memorable falls for us. There was a massive and ill-advised food fight in the cafeteria after the first home game. USC came into town in October, and I got to see the Irish beat them for the very first time. Notre Dame completed their pre-game warmups in their Navy blue home jerseys, and then found Kelly green jerseys, which ND had not worn since the 1940s, waiting for them in the locker room.

Wearing those green jerseys, the players then poured out of a huge wooden Trojan horse that had been constructed behind Carroll Hall (isolation is good for that sort of secretive thing). ND went on to a huge beatdown of USC, and the students went nuts. We tore down the goalposts.

It was a remarkable year on campus, because of the national championship. Joe Montana's junior year in a storied college career, with his legendary NFL career still ahead of him. Absolute studs like Ross Browner and Luther Bradley were in their last year, as well. I remember walking down a staircase in O'Shaugnessy Hall and my head was even with Ross Browner's, even though he was two stairs below me.

These were heady times for a Notre Dame freshman, and they set up expectations that are pretty unreasonable. For a while I fully expected Notre Dame to win a national championship once a decade, and thought that every Notre Dame class had the "right" to see them win once in their four years. These have not come to fruition; the last time ND won a national championship was in 1988 (Dan and I were there to see them beat West Virginia in the Fiesta Bowl). I have not been back to a game in a while. The ND football experience has become commercialized and over-hyped, in my opinion. Like some other things about Notre Dame, I prefer to remember it as it was, and to remember the good parts.

In November the trees turned bare, and by December or January the land and trees were covered in snow and the lake was frozen, so much so that we could walk across it as a shortcut back to the dorm. The campus was beautiful in winter, especially at night, with the Dome lit golden over a muted ivory landscape. I can remember walking across campus at night in winter, crossing the quad in front of the Dome, with huge snowflakes falling silently and gently around my head and shoulders. A feeling of peace and certainty, that there was a purpose to all this and there were people you loved and valued and who had your back at this place. That you were in this together. And that this place had had the same effect on my Dad.

Hawk on Carroll's front lawn, fall break 1978. In winter 1977 we sculpted a "hook 'em horns" in honor of ND's Cotton Bowl win over Texas.

Snow. Terry and I had never really seen that much of it before. Just at Mt. Waterman, when my parents took us to sled and throw snowballs, and at a Boy Scout winter camp, Camp Conrad, where my dad taught me the winter stars, the ones I still know the best (who doesn't know Orion?) and where my dad fell on an icy walkway, broke his elbow and got bursitis later in life because of it. So when it first snowed at Notre Dame, in late

1977, Terry and I went out on the front lawn of Carroll in our underwear, to experience it. The idiots from California.

And that winter we experienced PLENTY of it. The most snow in the history of Notre Dame. A blizzard charged through northern Indiana in late January, picking up moisture from Lake Michigan (if I ever write a novel it will be called Lake Effect) and absolutely dumping it, offloading it, in northern Indiana. So much so that Notre Dame closed for three days! Notre Dame, which had been around since 1842, had never closed due to weather. But for three days the campus was closed. The only vehicles moving on Highway 31, behind Carroll, were half-track Army vehicles. Classes were canceled; professors stayed in town. We students…made good use of our new-found free time.

We decided to hold a Blizzard Party. Of course, we couldn't drive to get alcohol. Only a couple Carroll guys had cars, mainly Tom Rumely and Bob Hogan (who famously owned the "Monte", his Monte Carlo). But driving was out. About 40 inches of snow had fallen and no roads were open at all. The conditions called for an expedition on foot, a trek. The liquor stores, like King's Cellar, were east of campus; we were on the west end. It became an undertaking not unlike a polar expedition, Franklin's attempt to reach the South Pole. A bunch of us suited up and grabbed backpacks, a makeshift sled. We set out, and it took us quite a while to make our way as we took turns breaking trail in the snow. Backpacks crammed with alcohol, we made it back and pulled off the party, which became really the first of the Carroll happy hours. Over the years we perfected this approach, and held semi-regular happy hours on Friday afternoons, for which Carroll became well-known. I remember going with Hogan to a liquor store and buying close to $400 of alcohol for one of these. Hey, we needed SOME incentive for women to make it out to Carroll! During the blizzard, with no classes to attend, we also played a massive game of snow football on Carroll's front lawn. Then we pretty much all got the flu. Guys would bring huge vats of orange juice back to the hall for the infirm.

Florida! Left, Action, OB, Mik and Lou Mal at Disney World. Middle, I'm with Dutch, Swegle and OB at the El Morocco in Daytona Beach. Right, Hogan and Action.

Spring at Notre Dame, as I think it is for any college in the Midwest or East, is remarkable and certainly not taken for granted. And it's pretty late in arriving. It's not like the snow disappears and then everything is green. It's a much more gradual and frustrating process, with lots of mud, even frozen mud, and dead brown grass. But you know spring is coming, and you deserve it, because you lived through a northern Indiana winter. Of course, you could jump the gun and drive to Florida for spring break. Which I did sophomore and senior years. It was a 20-plus hour drive, but Florida had things to offer that northern Indiana couldn't. Disney World. Warm beaches. Saltwater. Bare skin.

Spring took a more winding road to northern Indiana, but the time after spring break was just magic. Gradually the winter lessened its grip and allowed us to play softball and baseball, and hang out outside, on Carroll's big lawn. In spring I would hang out on that lawn, and coeds, enjoying the spring weather, would do so closer to the lake. Senior year I had a date with Theresa Schilling, who had been doing just that, and she complained to me that guys from Carroll had been hitting gold balls close to her that afternoon. Seems I had heard that from the guys, not knowing it was my date...

Because of its isolation and infrastructure, Carroll lent itself well to bonding among its inmates. Now, being a biologist, I know how evolution proceeds in isolated situations. Shit gets weird. Take Australia, where evolution occurred in isolation from other continents for hundreds of millions of years. And produced marsupials. It occurs to me that we were the marsupials of Notre Dame. Slightly, but fundamentally, different from the other mammals. We didn't mix that well with others (and still don't; at Notre Dame class reunions, I know less people than those who lived on the main part of campus). We tended to travel in a large group, because there was safety in numbers. Herd mentality. It was tribal, as you might say today. Brothers in arms. We had each other's back; it was us against the world.

The large central staircase at Carroll also brought us together, because everyone had to go up and down that staircase. In later years they got rid of that and installed staircases at either end. Not the same at all.

We had a healthy disrespect for authority. The illegal canoe. Liberating Colonel Bulmer's sign at the ROTC building, time and time again, in a clear sign of peaceful protest against...I don't know what the fuck it was against. The Vietnam War was long over. Scoffing at the no kegs in the dorm policy (it was amazing that a pony keg could fit in Rumely's backpack). RA's at Carroll had to adjust or pick fights all year. And we went through four rectors in four years; Dutch claims each experienced a slow descent into madness. Maybe not so slow, in a couple cases. Terry told me our great assistant rector, Fr. John Riedy, was apprehensive about being assigned to Carroll, because of the dorm's reputation. However, we absolutely loved Fr. Riedy, who was head of the university's Ave Maria Press. He was a great homilist, one of the best I've had to pleasure to listen to, and his view on life was so reasonable. He appreciated good food and wine, and once said, in a homily, that not every instance of premarital sex was a sin. Really?! Well, okay, then.

And, we abolished parietals. You've probably never heard of parietals. At the time, in the late 1970s, Notre Dame, being the conservative Catholic university that it was, had a policy of "in loco parentis". Which was Latin or Sanskrit or Mandarin or Mandan Sioux for "in the absence of parents", meaning that since your parents aren't here at school, we, the university, will act like them. And parietals was the policy that prevented you from having persons of the opposite sex in your dorm overnight (Notre Dame has all single-sex dorms), a policy which, of course, we found to be bullshit of the highest degree. So our hall council abolished the parietals, an act which had no legal or practical meaning whatsoever, didn't change a thing, but got good local press and was seen as an act of protest. Abolishing parietals is still high on my list of accomplishments.

In our relentless search for knowledge and enlightenment, or because we were bored, we discovered the steam tunnels junior year. Buildings at Notre Dame are, or at least were, heated by steam which travels from the power plant on the north edge of campus through underground pipes to different buildings on the main part of campus, and those pipes were in an underground tunnel system, accessible for maintenance. I'm not sure where we heard of it – may have been Action's older brother – but we learned of a steam tunnel entrance over near the liberal arts building. We entered it one night, started following it lord knows where. At the end of one tunnel was a half-door, which opened into the men's bathroom of the South Dining Hall!

This was momentous, because we suddenly had access to half the cafeteria food on campus. This was before alarm systems and cameras and motion detectors; there's no way this would happen today. A larger group of us went back the next week. Fall break was coming up and we needed victuals. We took bread, large cuts of sandwich meat, whatever we could carry that wouldn't be immediately missed. But we also fixed food in there, late at night – Terry fired up the grill and was making bacon! We made milkshakes! Some friends of ours from a woman's dorm found out about it, and made perhaps even a bigger raid. The next time we went down there, the door to the dining hall was locked. Some people just won't let you have anything.

Carroll was a veritable rogue's gallery of characters. All smart as fuck; I often said that every other person at ND was a valedictorian or salutatorian. We were no exception. What made them so unique? That we were outcasts, misfits, from the beginning? Or that we had no upperclassmen to tell us what to do and what not to do? Here, in no particular order, are the Carrollites, the Vermin, I bonded with and remain close to 40-plus years down the line (pretty much everybody turned out to be empathetic, productive, contributing members of society, and good husbands):

Ed "Steady Eddie" Durbin, or Durbs, sometimes Sgt. Nick, from Oak Harbor, Ohio, a great baseball, basketball and softball player and loyal as fuck. Most likely to get into a fight at a bar. A fellow bio major, he not only went on to get his PhD in entomology (His undergrad insect collection was stellar) but then got his MD, and is living the good life as a gynecologist in South Bend, of all places. Ed, Action and I roomed together junior year. Road trips to Ohio, where we partied with big burly Tom Durbin, Ed's brother and future usher at Notre Dame Stadium, and Greg Dahr, Tom's equally big, affable friend. Played with Hawk on some great Bookstore Basketball teams, with names that would make many people cringe and blush. For example, "The Purple Pulsating Pillars of Passion and the Bulbous Mushroom Tips".

Tom "Action" Jackson of Denver, who switched from engineering to business freshman year (like many did). Great athlete; played volleyball for the Notre Dame club volleyball team with Hawk and me senior year. Was a member of the gymnastics club and had to occasionally be retrieved, drunk, from that club's parties where they played drunken crack-the-whip on the quad. Still has not forgiven me for setting him up with a date (she was cute! And a volleyball player!) for a screw-your-roommate dance. Liberated many things from campus that were clearly more valuable and served a greater purpose in Carroll. Was our hall mailman. Went to law school and became a prosecutor in Colorado, putting the bad guys away.

Kevin O'Brien, OB, from Canton, Ohio, played drums in the Notre Dame Marching Band, and was our window into that slightly strange world. Those guys partied, too. He also switched from engineering freshman year. He's probably the one who has aged the least. Was the keeper of the date pack, given to one of us who happened to have a date; included the self-titled Bread album, the ultimate in make-out music.

Bob Hogan. Holy shit. Where does one even start? Known for his perfect hair (as he would tell you). From tiny, rural Whitney Point in upstate New York, from which he drove the legendary Monte, the black Monte Carlo, out to ND every year. Bold. Would say anything to anybody, and still does. He and Hawk were thrown together as roommates freshman year. RA Chris McCabe tried to catch them smoking pot, but never quite could. Was remarkably successful with women. No doubt because of the hair, and the car. Huge Dallas Cowboys fan, so much so that he named one of his boys Dallas. I expected another to be named Cleveland, after the Indians, but I guess he didn't like them quite as much.

Dan Dutcher, Dutch, from Biddeford, Maine, introduced us all to language never before heard west of the Maine state line.

Duddedee. Trinkets and toys. Also introduced us to lobster rolls. Gained a sure spot in heaven for putting up with his freshman year roommate, who ultimately did not make it through ND; at age 31 the fellow was sentenced to a 5-year prison term for manipulating stock prices. Dutch became a lawyer himself and rose up through the NCAA, where he ran the D3 division.

Tom Swegle, was another West Coaster, from Bishop O'Dea in Seattle (funny how you remember some high school names). He, Mik, Action and OB all had singles on the fourth floor freshman year, where a certain amount of hijinks occurred largely unbeknownst to RA Chris McCabe. For example, they used the metal dorm room trashcans to flood the hallway floor, and then they skated down the hall. Seems Chris McCabe eventually DID find out about that. Tom went on to law school and had a successful, long career with DOJ.

Mik! Tom Mikula, from Allentown, Pennsylvania. Tall, rangy, and athletic, Mik was a great and strong runner; he and I used to run the lakes and the SMC nature trail. Great sense of humor. Came back from Christmas break with a ski lift ticket still attached to his ski jacket; the lift ticket said "I don't ski". Also went on to law school and practiced property law, with a good amount of pro bono work on conservation easements. He left us too soon, passing in 2013.

Hawk! The Big Guy! Our one true celebrity in Carroll – what was he doing with us? Kevin Hawkins, from LA, was on the Irish basketball team and came from Notre Dame hoops royalty; his dad was Tommy Hawkins, who played for the Irish and the Lakers. And Hawk was an even better volleyball player, in my opinion. He absolutely anchored the Notre Dame club team I played on senior year. Had no problems socially; his single dorm room was known as the Boneyard. Had a sign on the door that said "The Doctor Is In". In later years Hawk became an absolute beacon of love, even an ordained minister, and beloved by our whole class of '81. Has been so many things to so many people, as they say.

Joey, the Italian Stallion, Joe Massaro from Fredericktown, Ohio. Home of the Fredtown Freddies, for whom Joe starred as quarterback. Was a year behind us in school, but hung out with us. Had a small TV, which Hawk borrowed quite a bit of the time ("Hey Joe, borrow your TV, man?"). Joey has been with a steel company for decades, and is now vice president. Named a son after a character in a movie.

Ah, the Great Pumpkin, Rums, Tom Rumely from Indiana. Known for his large red Afro-type hair. Great athlete – basketball, tennis, volleyball, natural leader, loud voice. Taught me SO much. Meat's meat and a man's gotta eat.

Chris Stoughton from Cleveland, easily one of the smartest people I've ever met. Physics major, ran "Food Sales", the late night dorm pizza outlet. Which provided quarts of Carling Black Label beer the night of the SMC panty raid. Held weekly study sessions prior to the dreaded Friday morning Emil T. Hofman quizzes, and correctly predicted quiz questions 90% of the time. Brought the infamous canoe to Carroll. Has studied astrophysics and cosmology at the Fermilab for a long time, and is the only one of us who truly understands that not only is the universe expanding, but that expansion is also speeding up. Makes my problems look small.

Other "regional" specialties: Mike Tanner, the "Mouth from the South", from Shreveport, whose freshmen roommate was Southside Johnny Wilmott from New Jersey. Lou Malveezi, "Chairman Mal" from Memphis, Big Jim from Louisville who roomed with Triet Tran from Vietnam.

Dan arranged for Terry to preside over funeral rites for the Carroll Hall happy hour in 1984.

Terry had his own unique Notre Dame experiences. He was perhaps better connected with the rest of campus. Freshmen year he sang in the well-known Notre Dame Glee Club, and he spent sophomore year in Maynooth, Ireland, with Notre Dame's Ireland abroad program. Which was actually run by SMC, and had plenty of SMC women. Tom Swegle was also in that Ireland program. Terry was barely able to convince my dad that he should go to Ireland for the program, my dad famously saying he did not want Terry "gallivanting around Europe". As it was, Terry did not go the Continent that year, but did plenty of gallivanting. He came back at Christmas with long curls and having given his hand-knit Irish sweater to an Irish girl, Marian, who I think was convinced she was Maureen O'Hara to Terry's John Wayne.

Students came back from abroad studies with their horizons considerably broadened, and some found ND life difficult to adjust to. I don't think Terry has ever had any problem adjusting to anything. Once at Notre Dame he decided to go talk to the university president, Ted Hesburgh (who was president of ND when my dad went there, too). It was rumored that if you climbed the fire escape and knocked on his office window at night, he'd let you in. Terry did this and they had a discussion about parietals. Not that it changed anything.

My brother Dan was a freshman at ND when Terry and I were seniors, and I believe he was the first prospective student ever to request to live in Carroll Hall, which he did based on our experiences there. And his Carroll cohort turned out be to even crazier than ours. Dan fit in right from the beginning. At the first happy hour we had that year, we convinced a woman friend of ours to sidle up to him and get friendly. Dan immediately put his arm around her and said, "How are you doing, honey?" I knew right then he was going to have a great four years.

At the end of Dan's senior year, the university banned alcohol in the dorm rooms. This spelled the end of the Carroll happy hour, and Dan got Terry, who was then in the novitiate at Notre Dame, studying to be a priest, to come preside at a funeral for the tradition. Terry led graveside services and then the men of Carroll buried the typical happy hour accoutrements in a hole in the ground behind Carrol. In a now unmarked gravesite. There are so many notable gravesites at Notre Dame.

To this day, there isn't anything I wouldn't do for these Carroll guys. We have showed up for football games, reunions, weddings (well, two of those were my weddings), one funeral, and one ordination. And one big birthday party. In 2019 Dan organized a birthday party to end all birthday parties, a surprise for Terry and my 60th, and he convinced these guys to come out to El Segundo for it. I don't think they needed that much convincing. I was shocked to see them there. Best present anyone has EVER given me, outside of the gift of attending Notre Dame, which my parents gave to me. Forever grateful for that.

Carroll Hall (plus a few honorary members) showed up for Hogan's wedding, Terry's ordination, and a 60th birthday party.

Lest you think it was all fun and games, let me assure you that I had a great academic experience at Notre Dame. First of all, I'll be up front: I pretty much got my butt kicked there academically. I came in with high hopes, or at least some thought, of going on to med school, to become the type of humanitarian doctor that ND grad Tom Dooley had become. Again, those delusions of grandeur. I was quickly disabused of that notion. My freshman year I found both biology and chemistry classes to be difficult, though I liked biology, my intended major, immensely. The general chemistry was that Emil T. Hofman class with his weekly quizzes, on which I didn't do that well, despite living next door to Chris Stoughton. Sophomore year on the pre-med track one takes organic chemistry, a butt-kicker of a class which is used to separate the wheat from the chaff. Though I passed that, I knew I was not in the same league as the true pre-meds, and I decided just to become, as I called it, a mellow biology major. My real interest lay in wildlife biology, which Notre Dame didn't offer. Its biology department was strong in microbiology, which did not excite me; I could not see myself wearing a lab coat all my life. But Notre Dame was also strong in ecology, the study of the relationships among plants, animals, and their environments. Now we were on to something.

Turns out the ND ecology program was well-established, and well-known. Robert Smith, the old ecology prof, had written his own textbook and was heavily influenced by C. Hart Merriam and F. C. Clements, Midwesterners who established the concepts of ecological succession and life zones. Aquatic ecology, in particular, was strong at Notre Dame, and I enjoyed that class, which had us sampling in nearby lakes and streams. Botany was taught by Fr. Joseph McGrath, a character who had studied kelp at UC Santa Barbara for his doctorate. He told of waiting for a wave to recede, then rushing out with a hatchet to hew at a kelp plant before the next wave came in. He took us into Chicago, which he told us was named by native Americans for the wild onions, or leeks, that grew there, to see the arboretum but also to get deep-dish pizza at Gino's East.

I began to focus in on what I really wanted to study in-depth. In an animal behavior class, I first began to think of birds as study subjects. There was one student in that class, Paul Broughton (the Irish leprechaun mascot!) who was a really good birder and knew all the birds on a walk around the campus. Very impressive. Eventually I would become like that, as well, studying American kestrels for my master's degree and conducting studies of bird communities in Texas and at the Channel Islands. But for the ND animal behavior class, I wanted to know, for a class project, what determined the populations swings of birds. Professor Eck gently, or maybe not so gently, told me that was impossible to do in a two-month time period. My grad advisor at Northern Arizona University told me the same thing when I proposed doing that for American kestrels, over a two-years master's thesis time period. But finally, at Channel Islands National Park, I was able to help determine what drove populations of endangered island foxes. Granted, it took more than two months or two years. More like five years. But at ND these seeds were sown. No higher calling for me than to determine what made animal populations tick, especially those of rare or endangered species, and then to use that information to conserve those species.

The other academic influence that changed me for the better was a writing class I took freshman year, as part of ND's freshman year of studies. Moira Baker taught the class, and she considerably strengthened my writing, curing me of some bad habits – such as my overuse of the dash. In fact, when I look back at all the things I learned in high school, college and grad school, the most important might be critical analysis and cogent writing. The ability to write served me well in 30 years as a biologist, and set me apart from others. Cathy and I even wrote a book about island foxes. Sometimes I think that it doesn't matter what you did in science, if you can't write it up.

The family flew back to ND to see us graduate in May, 1981. Last hurrah in Carroll for us...

What did I leave Notre Dame with? Everything that propelled me forward. A sense of place, a recognition that places are important, and need to be preserved. That we have a stewardship responsibility for those places (National Park Service, anyone?). An appreciation for the beauty in this world. A healthy disrespect for authority. Lifelong friendships, and a loyalty to these people, my Notre Dame cohort, that defies time and distance and keeps me coming back to campus when I can but also, more importantly, compels me to check in on these folks regularly. I refuse to let those connections die or stagnate. They're too important to me. We are all still in this together, some 40 years later.

Notre Dame has changed of course, in those 40 years, and not all of those changes are for the better. ND football is commercialized. Campus is crowded with new buildings. And I despise the fact that ND invited Mike Pence to speak at graduation, and Bill Barr addressed the law school. In doing so, Notre Dame honored and conferred credibility on the most un-Christian and arguably evil of any presidential administration. Maybe one day I will get over that, and recognize that the good of Notre Dame, the Tom Dooley and Tom Coonan part, outweighs the other. Terry says he goes back there often in his mind, and recalls the better parts of it. Yes. It was about something, indeed. Go Irish.

Turnpikes and Tollroads

From northern Indiana we took the great interstates of the northeast, I80 and I90, through Ohio and Pennsylvania and New York, to our eventual East Coast destination, Worcester, Massachusetts. As in Indiana, these roads crossed great rolling fields of corn and other crops and grasses, the miles marked by farmsteads and windbreaks and rest areas and the ever-present Stuckey's (I sometimes think Stuckey's did more to settle this country and achieve manifest destiny than did the railroads). There were occasional sedge-lined ponds, and small groves of the native trees that had once covered great swaths of this land. Now all, or most, had been sacrificed to John Deere and International Harvester. It's said that a squirrel could once jump from branch to branch all the way from the East Coast to the Mississippi. Though I don't know why it would've wanted to. There must have been acorns everywhere.

I remember seeing those farmhouses, by themselves on the corners of large farms, and wondering what it would be like to grow up there. A barn and silo, yard cluttered with farm equipment. No doubt muddy in the spring (I didn't yet know what mud rooms were). Nearest neighbor kid a long ways away. Simple two-story white clapboard farmhouses buffeted by winter winds and weather, and you still had to go out to the barn and feed the horses and the chickens. But it also must have been a life closer to the land than my suburban one, and I think I envied those farm kids a little.

I'm thinking Mom was justifiably nervous as we clambered onto the guardrail above Niagara Falls.

Some of these highways were toll roads – you had to PAY to use them. A foreign concept; we didn't (as of yet) have those in California. But it became a ritual to which we looked forward. Rolling up to the toll booth, one of us kids would get to roll down our window and throw the change in the basket. Very satisfying sound as the coins slid down and tinkled into the machine. Not unlike a putt dropping into the bottom of the cup.

So we followed the big 18-wheelers across the top of the East, along the shores of Lake Erie and Lake Ontario. The Great Lakes, one of the most prominent geographical features of North America. What gave those lakes the right to be so huge, dwarfing any other lake on the continent? I mean when does the term lake give way to inland sea? If you can't see across it, I think the term lake is a little inadequate as a descriptor, no? Several times, we traveled ABOVE Lake Erie, in Canada, to get to the Northeast. Canada! A different country! How exotic. We took in Niagara Falls, peering way down into the chasm as the Maid of the Mist, tiny from up at the top, bobbed in the water at the bottom of the falls. Niagara Falls, the St. Lawrence, the Great Lakes…these are lakes and rivers writ large, almost ridiculously so. Paul Bunyan-esque.

In Ohio, we passed near towns where my future Notre Dame buddies lived. Funny to think they were living parallel kids' lives as we drove by in those summers. Were their lives like those of Homer Price, in Robert McCloskey's Centerburg Tales? A middle American, Norman Rockwell-type existence? Or darker yet, as in Sherwood Anderson's Winesburg, Ohio? They were probably having typical Little League summers. But I'd like to think they went to fishing holes, in cutoffs, and swung out over the water on ropes. Ed told me of a game they played: mailbox baseball. The passenger in a slowly driving vehicle would lean out and take healthy swings at mailboxes along rural roads. Batter up. Not sure if they actually did any cow-tipping, though.

Our route along I90 hugged Lake Erie, passing through Cleveland, and Erie, Pennsylvania on its way to Buffalo and Rochester. Home of ND guys. Cannot imagine winters on that side of Lake Erie, no doubt even colder and deeper than South Bend winters. I90 traverses New York state above the Finger Lakes region; alternatively, we could take 86 and 88 below it. A beautiful area of glacier-carved lakes, seemingly made by a giant hand raking across the land. Heavily wooded rocky gorges leading to them (in that region they were "gorges", not "canyons"). My daughter Bridget chose this area for college, attending Ithaca College in the town of that name, at the bottom of Lake Seneca. Ithaca is "gorges", as they say. How can you not like a place called Buttermilk Falls?

My dad remembers upstate New York as just green, so different from where we lived. On one trip we had a flat tire and pulled over to the side of the road. There was a guy mowing the grassy slope above the side of the road, grass that grew without being watered! He came down the slope and switched out the tire for us. And he made us all walk up the slope and safely away from the highway while he did it. Dad says he refused to take anything for his efforts. The kindness of strangers. It was also in upstate New York that my sister Nora asked Dad if he knew the way home.

The Clan

Crossing the state line between New York and Massachusetts put us in western Mass, on the Mass Pike, cutting through rolling, wooded hills which were much more thickly wooded prior to European contact, when it was inhabited by the Mohicans and Wampanoags. This land was tribal for us, too. It was home to the Clan, the large, all-encompassing, Irish-American family of my dad's, whose relatedness to us was bewildering. Coonans, Campbells, Husseys, Hehirs, Crottys, Conlins, Coynes…to this day I have to ask my dad how we're related to certain folks. And sometimes he has to look it up, himself.

Long ago, in the old country (that would be Ireland), a certain John Coonan married Bridget Boland, and they left for America. They were my dad's great grandparents. John Coonan ended up farming the rocky New England soil, and giving his name to a number of descendants. Bridget Coonan, my dad's great grandmother, is whom I named my daughter Bridget after, though there is an alternate story. You see, it could be that I named Bridget after Bridget Adargo, one of the hottest girls in my freshman class at St. Bernard's High. Maybe I figured it couldn't hurt for my daughter to have a hot name. Not that I told Cathy that story. We're going with the great-great-great grandmother one. So much more respectable.

My dad was born in Worcester in 1934, but in fact his parents, Frederick Leo Coonan and Anna Hussey Coonan, were living in Annapolis, Maryland at the time, where my grandfather taught metallurgy, at the Naval Postgraduate School of the Naval Academy. My grandmother, Nana, was a nurse, professionally, and decided to go home to Worcester to have the baby, at the hospital where she had practiced. So while my dad was born in Worcester, he didn't consider that home; home was Annapolis. Which was unusual for the Clan; most family members stayed right there in Worcester, if not Massachusetts. Being in California, we were some of the farthest-flung family members. For most Clan members, Worcester and New England was their anchor and their home. For some others, like my dad, it was a place of roots, a place to be from, and a good place, at that; a place you could return to, and be welcomed by the Clan.

Just as Nana had returned home to Worcester to have my dad, so had she returned there by the time we started our visits, in the 1960s. The Naval Postgraduate School moved from Annapolis to Monterey, California, in 1952, my dad's senior year in high school. My grandfather (we called him Pop), drove out to Monterey after Christmas, and the rest of the family stayed in Annapolis so my dad could finish his senior year of high school. Dad says it was terrible watching his father drive away on a cold, rainy day after Christmas that year. They would not see him again until graduation, in May. They put the house up for sale and it sold quickly, too quickly; Nana, Dad, Ted and Pat moved into an apartment for the spring. After Dad's graduation they all headed out to Monterey; at the end of that summer, my dad flew to Notre Dame.

In Monterey they lived on 17-Mile Drive, and I vaguely remember visiting Nana and Pop there as a very young child. I remember that Pop smoked a pipe (Dad did, for a while, too), and was a good artist; he painted a pig (also smoking a pipe) on the crib Terry and I shared up there. I also distinctly remember

Mom hiding a Dramamine pill in a spoonful of strawberry jam so we wouldn't get carsick on the drive back down Highway 1. God, I hated those Dramamine pills. And the liquid was even worse.

Dad's parents: Nana (Anna Hussey) and Pop (Frederick L. Coonan).

Pop had lung problems, emphysema to be exact, and I hear or remember that he had a tank of oxygen at the house. These problems must have been severe. He passed away in 1961, while we were visiting, due to a lung infection; and I can't imagine how that must have been for his family. Dad says he was devastated. Nana moved back to Worcester, her birthplace and home of the Clan, sometime thereafter. Nana lived in an apartment at 49 Goldthwaite Road (again, one of those addresses wood-burned in my mind). It was an upstairs apartment in a building that stood by itself, with a rocky New England hill right behind it. We loved that hill, and spent much time there. Throwing rocks at each other. New England may have been too rocky for good farming, but for rock-throwing it was ideal.

The apartment was accessed by a long indoor stairway, which I found confusing. Which was the front door? The outside door at the bottom? Or the indoor door at the top of the stairs? It was perhaps my first experience with an apartment, and it was impressionable. In fact, weirdly, when I read the Sherlock Holmes stories a few years later I imagined 222B Baker Street as Nana's apartment, with an indoor stairway leading to the second story residence, and a picture window overlooking the street. Though it's admittedly hard to substitute the suburban, leafy streets of Worcester for the grimy urban lanes of late 19th Century London.

Eventually Nana moved from Goldthwaite Road to 21 Shattuck Street, to a flat above that of her sister Betty. Here's where the dynamics of the Clan appear in sharp relief. Nana had two sisters, Mary and Betty, and two brothers, Dan and Frank. Dan was in oil (Standard of New Jersey) and Frank became Fr. Frank, a Jesuit missionary who served overseas, in Baghdad, for many years (and before that gentle land was torn by strife). As notable as these two Hussey males were, it was the women who ran the family. If you've ever doubted that matriarchy is our natural order, take a look at the Husseys, and the Clan. Life in all of Worcester seemed to swirl around the three Hussey sisters and their families.

Nana's two sisters had married two brothers, Eddy and Leo Hehir. I always wondered how that came to be. A double date gone awry? Was it a double wedding? Were they each other's best men, and maids of honor? Leo was a fireman (a traditional Irish-American occupation, like the railroad men of my Midwestern relatives), and Eddy, according to Dad, went door-to-door selling insurance. And collecting premiums. Which sounds awfully like an Irish protection racket.

Nana lived at 21 Shattuck Street, in a "flat' above her sister Betty. Her grandkids, shown in 1976, included Jenny and Megan Hackett.

Eddy and Mary and their children (Franny, Marty, and Sally) and Leo and Betty plus kids (Dick, Tom and Mike) formed the white-hot core, the nucleus of the Clan. Nana and Pop had not lived in Worcester in years, and two of their three kids (my dad and Uncle Ted) had left long, long ago. Their sister Pat eventually came back to live in Worcester. The Hussey sisters, their kids and husbands, their grandchildren…the Clan was enormous. And hard to conceptualize, get a handle on, especially for kids from California. At a Clan Fourth of July celebration in 1972, my brother Dan turned to my mom and said, "Who are all these people?" My mom replied that they were our relatives. Dan then said, "So why haven't I met any of them before?" And birth order was everything. After moving back to Worcester, Nana was required to call her older sister, Mary, every day.

The Clan was very Irish, and very Catholic. You can hardly distinguish between the two, in this case. Nana's younger brother was a Jesuit, and worshiped by the family. Many of the Clan had attended one of the local Catholic colleges, Holy Cross and Assumption. The Catholicism was just a given. Though the later expose of priest sexual abuse soured some of the Clan; my Aunt Pat and Uncle John shifted to alternative Catholic churches, which rejected the top-down authority of the Church and some of its more repugnant teachings (on gays and birth control, for example).

At Lake Quinsigamond's Washington Club, we swam and drank orange sodas, while the elders held court.

At one time or another, we saw most of the Clan at the Washington Club, which sounds a lot more high-end than it was. The Club comprised a clubhouse and some lakefront on Lake Quinsigamond, in Worcester. What a great name, Lake Quinsigamond. Face it, our country would be pretty boring without Native American names, one of my favorites being Pottawatomi, a name appropriated for a zoo in South Bend. The clubhouse at the Washington Club was a dark and dank one-room cement structure where you could change, and buy a soda at the soda machine. The rocky and grassy lakefront was just that. And we loved the place. What's better than a lake in the summertime? If it seemed as though there only Clan members at the Washington Club, that's because it was mostly so. Solely Worcester Irish-Americans belonged there, the actual ownership and club entry rules being murky. Apparently the Italians had their own club on Lake Quinsigamond.

All we required was water in which to swim. The occasional horseflies, which were huge, would buzz in and hover around our heads, full of ill intentions. Sometimes we'd fish, trying to catch crappy little lake fish with balls of white bread, led by my dad's cousin Mike Hehir. The older generation – Nana, Mary and Betty, who would now be called the Council of Elders by the Clan – would hold court in lawn chairs, scarves tied around their heads, as two generations buzzed around them.

I was impressed by two great swimmers in the family: my dad's sister Pat, and his cousin Tommy Hehir, who was smart and charismatic and ended up a Harvard professor, leading the charge for accessibility, especially in education. Both Tommy and Pat had strong bodies and were capable of swimming far, and fast.

And if the new station wagon was the ostensible reason for our 1967 trip, Pat was solely the reason for our trip in 1969. In fact that year my dad had made reservations for us at some June Lake cabins, but his sister decided to marry her fiancé, John Hackett, before he shipped off to Germany with the Army. So, no June Lake (ever; we never went there); Springfield Lake and Lake Quinsigamond would suffice instead, on our cross-country trip to see Pat marry John.

They were married at St. Joan of Arc church, with my dad walking her down the aisle, in Pop's absence. The wedding was presided over by a Fr. Texar, who later ended up in prison, thanks to the long-overdue exposure of sexual abuse by Catholic priests. At the wedding Mass, congregants received communion under both species, meaning both bread and wine (the biologist in me takes some issue with the use of that term). 20-year old Tommy Hehir was a eucharistic minister offering congregants a sip of wine, and was tasked with finishing the wine after communion. I remember him tilting his head far back to drain the chalice, to an audible gasp from his mother, Aunt Betty. Hey, get the job done.

In 1969 Dad's sister Pat married John Hackett.

The reception was held at Holy Cross College on one of the seven hills of Worcester. My sister Katie, four years old at the time, caused a stir when she found the light switch and turned off the lights to the entire reception. I remember being busted by dad's cousin Franny for picking the cashews out of a bowl of mixed nuts. Which is something I still do.

John Hackett. Talkative – he and Pat were counselor/social worker types – and acerbic, he always claimed he would never have "tenure" in the family, because he wasn't a blood relative. Which was true, and we reminded him of that, mercilessly, all the time. John, who did not lack for opinions, especially about subjects such as the shortcomings of the Catholic Church and the tendency of certain family members to buy "designer dogs", originated the concept of "Deck Talk", where family members would sit around and talk about "how the pigs eat the slop". Dan morphed this into "Dock Talk", which became the primary activity (no fishing or water skiing) we engaged in at Lake Almanor.

In 1976 Terry, Dan and I flew to Boston while the rest of the family drove out. Apparently, this allowed Dan to finish his baseball season and not miss out on a family trip. This was the first time I had ever flown (the second time would be when Terry and I flew to Notre Dame freshman year; Katie says Mom cried for 4 days straight and wore sunglasses to school to hide her puffy eyes) and it was high adventure, beginning with the kid on the plane, Yanni, who WOULD NOT SHUT UP.

Pat and John picked us up and squired us around Massachusetts for a week or so. We did everything. We attended a Boston Pops concert. We went to a Red Sox game in venerable Fenway Park (a deputy director of the National Park Service once told me he thought that Fenway and Wrigley belonged in the National Park system, along with Graceland). That night was memorable. It was the night Tom Yawkey, long-time owner of the Red Sox, passed away, and Red Sox icon and Hall of Famer Carl Yastremski hit a three-run homer to beat the Milwaukee Brewers. By this time Terry and I were closet Red Sox fans and Terry had even bought an 8mm movie, with no sound, of the classic Red Sox – Reds World Series of the previous year. Carlton Fisk waving his home run fair in the immortal sixth game.

Dad's cousin Tommy Hehir and his buddy Tony took us into Boston for the day, where we ate crepes for lunch and pizza in the North End for dinner, the latter at the now-shuttered European Restaurant, greeted, as I recall, by a maître d in a green suit. Who may have still been there when I ate at that restaurant 40 years later. That's the way I recall it, anyway. Dan remembers the pizza as being excellent, and he loved walking the Freedom Trail with Tommy and Tony, seeing the Old North Church and Paul Revere's house. Tommy and Tony were two good-looking, athletic young men and Tommy's mother, Aunt Betty, couldn't understand why they hadn't yet found nice young women to marry. Turns out there was a very good reason for that. They didn't like girls, so much.

The Paul Revere statue and Old North Church in Boston, and the Minuteman at Lexington made the American Revolution more real for us.

Massachusetts is where we first ate lobster, another cataclysmic event for us Coonans, expanding our palates to beyond the pale. There was no going back to tuna burgers and tuna noodle casserole, as far as seafood was concerned. For lobster we drove out of Worcester to Sudbury, home of the Chez Ami restaurant, which specialized in lobster dinners. For about 4 bucks. Amazing! Maine lobster and baked potato. Uncle Eddy was known for eating EVERYTHING out of the lobster, including the green intestines and the eyeballs. Uncle Eddy also had to have franks and beans every Saturday night, and after he passed it was learned that he slept with a handgun under his pillow. Maybe in case Aunt Mary ever failed to make him franks and beans on a Saturday night.

I was fascinated by the intricate rigging and small decks of the USS Constitution ("Old Ironsides").

Just as we immersed ourselves in Lincoln lore in Springfield, so we dove into colonial history in Massachusetts. Concord and Lexington, where the ragtag colonials stood up to the redcoats, and Sturbridge Village, a re-creation of a colonial town. There living history enactors fired muskets and worked looms and made colonial treats, and we watched real pigs eat the slop. In Boston Harbor we toured the USS Constitution, Old Ironsides, veteran of the War of 1812 and symbol of American resilience against British aggression. The warship was surprisingly small – barely 200 feet in length; we could hardly stand up below decks. Later, I would put together a model of the ship, and it stood on my bedroom shelf for a number of years. I shared a love of sailing vessels, or at least the idea of them, with my dad, who had grown up on Chesapeake Bay in the shadow of the Naval Academy. Like him, though, I was prone to seasickness.

Which is a little ironic, because I spent plenty of time on boats, going to and from the Channel Islands, during my time as a wildlife biologist there. Never really developed any sea legs, though. And there were some rough passages at times. Heading into heavy seas, with waves "stacked up" by Santa Ana winds… good lord. At least on the return trip the wind and the seas were at your back. And sometimes it was pure glass out there. Pods of common dolphins, several thousand strong, would race over to the boat and surf in the bow and stern waves. Never got tired of that! Saw humpback and blue whales, though both were rare sightings for the park boats. The best encounter was with orcas. We were returning from Anacapa Island and surprised some orcas which had just killed a seal (there is one family pod of orcas in the Southern California Bight, and they are seen up and down the Los Angeles and Ventura County coasts). These orcas were not pleased that we had interrupted their lunch. The big male made a series of charges at the boat, passing underneath each time. We were actually with a whale biologist, who had previously swum among orcas, but he said there was no way he'd get in the water with them that day.

In my youth, I had occasionally pictured myself on Navy vessels (daydream: Army or Navy? Marine Corps, Air Force? Navy, definitely) out of loyalty to my grandfather's connection to the Naval Academy and to my dad's affinity for the Navy. And I certainly don't share my dad's love of military history to the extent that Terry does. But if I had to pick a war and a theatre to study, it would be World War II's battle for the Pacific. And I certainly developed a love of seafaring explorers. I built a model of Sir Francis Drake's Golden Hind (and JFK's PT109, come to think of it), ate up Magellan and Da Gama, Saint Brendan, Leif Ericson. Read Mellville. I was fascinated with Captain James Cook, who opened Hawaii to the West, and his protégé, William Bligh, subject of a mutiny in the South Seas. Would I have joined Christian Fletcher in choosing to stay in Tahiti? Yeah, probably. But my stomach probably would not have allowed me to sail to Tahiti in the first place.

We visited Plymouth colony, site of that first European establishment, and one of the first European toeholds on the continent, a movement which, aided by disease and weapons, would spell doom for North American native peoples. There's a replica of the Mayflower there, and boy is it tiny, less than 100 feet in length. Columbus' three ships were also dinky, around 60 feet; amazing they were seaworthy enough to cross the Atlantic (aided of course, by the trade winds, which I teach my middle schoolers is an example of how geography determines history).

Our visits to the East Coast were thus an entrée for us into the origins of European settlement of the continent. A history that, I would much later learn, was Eurocentric and pretty much ignored the complex cultures that existed on this continent prior to European contact, and conveniently or willfully downplayed the extinction of those native peoples. My awareness of this would not be fully formed until much later in life. Still, the East coast, with its deeper history than that of southern California (our houses are not nearly as old!), sparked my interest in the story of land settlement and cultural development. A story that, we now know, not only cast aside the value of native peoples, but embraced and utilized racism to permanently subjugate Black people. Why does it take us so long to learn?

The Way Back

Sure, we could have returned from the East Coast the way we came. But what would be the fun in that? We were taking trails, as my dad would say. Even the Magi, the Three Kings, went back a different way, after they had achieved their objective of finding baby Jesus. Granted, they returned by a different route for security reasons. My childhood friend Rick Carr, whose brother was a Marine, used to say, "Get there, get it done, and get back." Which is as good a piece of advice as I've ever heard. Brings to mind the two major lessons I learned in 30 years of supervising for the NPS: get the job done, and treat your people well.

We had achieved our objective: we had visited family in Illinois and Massachusetts. Now it was time to see some shit. Our return from the East Coast differed in each of the four major trips we took. In 1967 we pretty much went straight back, with another stop in Springfield. My dad says Mom would cry for a full two states after we left Springfield the second time. The return trip in 1969, after Pat and John's wedding, took in Washington, D.C and environs. Which is monumental, literally. You HAVE to take your kids to see DC, just as you HAVE to take your kids to see the Grand Canyon. It's a required element in parenting.

So in 1969, after seeing the colonial sites in Boston, we continued our short course in American history by visiting

Washington, D.C. and Mount Vernon. Looking back at the photos, it seems very uncrowded. And of course, everything was relatively uncrowded then; there were less people in the country, less people traveling, and the bicentennial was some years away. A total of five people in my dad's picture of the reflecting pool and Washington Monument. Four people in front of the White House (and no double fence, no protesters).

In a relatively uncrowded Washington, D.C., in 1969, we took in the sites, including changing of the guard at the Tomb of the Unknown Soldier.

The Lincoln Monument impressed, with its giant statue of the sitting, wise and benevolent president, apparently contemplating the hard choices he had made to save the Union, decisions that took such a toll on him, physically. Lincoln's decision to wage war against the rebellious South as the latter chose states' rights and defense of barbaric slavery over preservation of the union, and Lincoln's decision to free slaves, were momentous and gargantuan, easily justifying the size of his memorial, and his place in American hearts. We now know it was an unfinished notion, as Blacks have continued to suffer the cruelty of racism long after they had been "freed" from slavery.

The changing of the guard at Arlington National Cemetery's Tomb of the Unknown was a quiet and somber affair, and long. The old guard and the new guard were both on scene together for some time, a point not lost on Bob Newhart, who explained to television wife Emily that it was sometimes like that in relationships, as well. She was not pleased to hear that.

In later years Cathy and I took the girls to D.C., because, again, that's one of the things you have to do as parents. D.C. was more crowded, for sure, but still awe-inspiring. Additional monuments had been erected since I had last visited. Maya Lin's Vietnam memorial was monolithic and somber, a (literally) deep experience as one contemplated the 55,000 American dead, who had died for…for what, exactly? I loved the FDR memorial (with his dog immortalized!), but the Korean War memorial was perhaps my favorite. A platoon of larger-than-life GIs slogging up a wet hillside, clearly tired and cold. Maybe accurately depicting the fog of war.

Southern Cooking

Washington was so close to DC, Dad's boyhood home, that we visited that city to take in the Naval Academy and see where Dad spent his formative years. Annapolis, a beautiful city, remains one of my dad's favorite places. The whole situation is a study in contrasts. Dad was born in Worcester, in the North, but grew up in Annapolis, in the South. Nana and Pop were Massachusetts through and through but transplanted to Maryland, where they lived for over 20 years.

Maryland was much warmer than Massachusetts; more humid, too. Dad learned to sail on the Chesapeake Bay in classes taught by the Naval Academy. He because a good boxer in a junior boxer program run by the Naval Academy. He loved life at 197 South Cherry, his boyhood home. There were no fences separating the back yards, and every year Bowie would come with a horse and a plow and dig furrows for gardens, along the length of the back yards. Victory gardens, of course, were standard during World War II, and Pop grew the usual, plus corn, and even tobacco and cotton, maybe a nod to the South. Dad took the cotton balls to school, to show the kids how hard it was to separate the cotton fiber from the seeds (Eli Whitney's cotton gin saved a lot of hands and backs, and also contributed to the rise of slavery by increasing demand for cotton).

Dad attended St. Mary's Academy, where he played football (guard and captain, like Terry) and lacrosse. Dad's upbringing in

Pop and Nana's house was strict. One time Dad went swimming at a class picnic even though Pop had told him not to. Pop could tell that he had, because Dad's pants were wet; Pop instructed Dad to go to the back yard and cut a switch, so that Pop could beat him. Apparently, the terror of cutting the instrument of your own punishment was enough. Pop didn't go through with it.

In Annapolis we saw Dad's boyhood home, and the nuclear subs at the Naval Academy. Dad was a fierce junior boxer at the Naval Academy.

Dad enjoyed a nice childhood in Annapolis. Nana and Pop allowed him and his younger brother Ted to bike all over town, to school and lacrosse practice, to the Naval Academy for sailing lessons. They could venture into the nearby woods (where they picked up ticks!) after checking with Nana and Pop. But life in Maryland was undeniably southern; it was segregated then, in the 40s and 50s. There were no Black students at St. Mary's Academy; they had their own, poorer high school. Blacks sat in a separate section of the church Dad attended. Blacks had their own drinking fountains in downtown Annapolis. Mom and Dad also encountered racism when they moved to Anniston, Alabama, right after getting married; Dad did a stint with the Army Chemical Corps as part of his obligation to the Army's Reserve Officer's Training Corps. Alabama is deep South, where the legacy of the "human stain" lingered longer. And likely still does.

It is hard for me to come to grips with this, having grown up in a diverse southern California in the 60s and 70s. In fact, my high school was much more diverse than Notre Dame. I had assumed, wrongly, that racism had been generally taken care of by the Civil War and emancipation, and the Civil Rights Act. Not nearly so. It surprised me to hear that racism existed even in Northern states. The Ku Klux Klan was very active in Indiana, and even had a run-in with Notre Dame students. Boston is notoriously racist. The Red Sox were the last baseball team to integrate, and several Black ball players have clauses in their contracts barring a trade to Boston; that is the only place they have been called the n-word to their faces. And of course, Minnesota. We remain a work in progress, don't we?

Pop had a great influence on my dad, who looked to him for guidance in many areas. As Dad was considering a career, Pop advised him to shy away from aircraft companies, whose fortunes rose and fell, and instead stick with petroleum or chemical companies. Pop certainly had the academic chops. His textbook, Principles of Physical Metallurgy, published in 1943, was used by over 20 schools and universities. Pop actually thought Dad should go on for a PhD, but Dad decided not to, having had enough of academia (and a less-than-ideal experience with his major adviser, for his master's program). Pop's death in 1961 was devastating to Dad; Pop had been my dad's support all his life, and to this day Dad misses Pop's advice and strength, and regrets that Pop did not live to enjoy the rest of our family. You can't overstate the influence of a dad on their children. As I mentioned, my dad is the finest man I ever known, a model that I still aspire to emulate. And fall quite short at times!

The High Water Mark

Terry became enamored of, perhaps even obsessed with, war games early on. He would buy board games that recreated famous battles and replay those battles, one of which was perhaps the most famous battle on American soil, Gettysburg. He even found like-minded people in the South Bay, well before social media made this easy to do. Before Terry could drive himself, Dad would drive Terry to meet war game enthusiasts for an afternoon of battle. Dad would take our dog Coley and walk her around while Terry waged war. Terry and my dad share a love of military history, and if you could see my dad's house you'd be impressed by the hundreds of military books he has (so many that we bought him another bookshelf, and created a spreadsheet for him to catalogue them).

Thus it was entirely natural that Dad took the family to Gettysburg on our 1972 trip, an again in 1976. It's a battle of great significance, and perhaps the most visited battle site in the US. Gettysburg is also the site of Lincoln's Gettysburg Address, one of the greatest pieces of prose ever written. At one time I had it memorized. Gettysburg National Battlefield is run well by the National Park Service, at that point my future employer, which sought to retain its historic character in the midst of development that naturally impaired it, and a tourist industry that is commercially motivated. See the story of the Gettysburg tower, a 300-foot metal tower build on private land outside the park and offering views into the park, at the price of being an ugly blight on the historic landscape. The NPS and the state fought the construction of the tower but lost, having no jurisdiction on private land. The longterm solution required passage of a law making the tower land part of the park. The NPS eventually was able to tear down the tower and compensate the former owners.

Terry dwarfed by General Meade's statue on Cemetery Ridge, 1976.

Dad gave Terry the Gettysburg war game for Christmas in 1971, so by 1972 we were well-acquainted with the story of the 3-day battle, and its details: the faceoff between the Confederates on Seminary Ridge and the Union forces on Cemetery Ridge; the bloody fighting at the Wheatfield and the Peach Orchard. Spangler's Spring. Big Round Top and Little

Round Top, where Colonel Joshua Chamberlain (Jeff Daniels to you movie watchers) famously conducted a wheel maneuver and fought off a Rebel charge. We even knew about Fr. Corby, a Notre dame priest who was a battlefield chaplain memorialized by a statue at Gettysburg ("Fair Catch Corby" is apparently signaling for a fair catch; you can't escape Notre Dame football, even on a battlefield). And, perhaps most significantly, we know about the field of Pickett's Charge, where George Pickett led a desperate Confederate attempt to break the Union line in half on the battle's third day. It failed, at the Bloody Angle, but not by much, and the Confederate advance marked the High Water Mark of the Confederacy, the farthest Rebel incursion into the North. It was downhill from there for the Confederates. Jeb Stuart's cavalry were missing in action during the battle, and may have tipped the advantage to the southerners had they been effective. But no. The South would eventually be defeated, and the Union restored. At a very high cost.

When I played the Gettysburg war game with Terry he always took the Confederate side, which was more challenging, since they had fewer forces (and he won, more often than not). On the 1972 trip Dad let Terry walk the field of Pickett's Charge, in the rain, starting what turned out to be a minor obsession. Terry walked from the Confederate position on Seminary Ridge to the Bloody Angle on Cemetery Ridge. Terry has since walked - or run – Pickett's Charge no less than eight times, taking his boys with them. In fact, Gettysburg is a regular vacation stop for Terry and his family, and a place of great significance for him. Terry asked Katia to marry him at Gettysburg in 2011. Terry went on to major in history at Notre Dame and get a masters in the same at Boston College, and I have no doubt that our Gettysburg stops help set him on that path. Considering the atrocities that surround the Civil War, it is entirely fitting that Terry works in the human rights field, fighting human trafficking – the modern version of slavery.

I got a little artistic taking pics of Gettysburg on our 1976 trip.

It is unsettling, at best, and horrific, at worst, to contemplate Americans killing Americans on American soil. The South fought to defend a way of life based on a barbaric practice of enslaving and brutalizing fellow humans, and took up arms against the United States. Today the generals and politicians that advanced the southern cause and slavery are rightly seen as terrorists and racists, and statues and Confederate flags are coming down as America comes to grip with its racist past and present. Indeed, the story of America is the story of racism, which has pervaded and persisted through all aspects of our history, since the slave trade brought the first Africans in 1619. Gettysburg remains a poignant and painful reminder of the struggle for true equality. Hallowed ground, as Lincoln said.

You Could Look It Up

If Gettysburg was influential and emblematic in Terry's life, then Cooperstown might have been the same for Dan. On our '76 trip Dad allowed us the choice of places to visit, and Dan chose Cooperstown, New York, site of the National Baseball Hall of Fame. Cooperstown is, in a word, idyllic, a charming small town in leafy upstate New York, accessible only by two-lane country roads. The location of the baseball hall of fame there is perfect, maybe evocative of a simpler time, when your heroes loomed larger than life, untarnished (to your knowledge) by scandal. The room with the actual plaques is quiet and reverential, like a church. Cooperstown, like Gettysburg, is hallowed ground of sorts, as Uncle John said of my return visit there in 2013, "Fall on your knees, for you have been on sacred ground."

Dan in front of Babe Ruth's locker at the hall of fame, in 1976; Carrie in front of Kershaw's locker at the hall in 2013.

Our family goes in for sports big-time, but Dan took it to another level. Arguably the best athlete in the family, he's the one who made All-Stars in Little League and Babe Ruth ball, and whose All-Star teams advanced the furthest. Dan played baseball (and football) in high school and became a pretty decent beach volleyball player. Moreover, sports became his life, his profession. Talk about doing what you love. He pivoted from commercial law to sports administration, volunteering as Notre Dame's compliance expert in their athletic department and parlaying that into a steady rise in athletic departments, including a stint as athletic director of Santa Clara University and head of the East Coast Athletic Conference. Follow your passion, and all done with integrity. Our visit to Cooperstown was a highlight, of all our trips, for Dan, who took pictures next to the lockers of the greats. My dad remembers seeing the Abbott and Costello routine on film there. Cathy and I stopped by there on a college tour for Bridget in 2013, and it was even better than I remembered. They even had an exhibit on the All-American Girls Professional Baseball League, of League of Our Own fame, yet another great baseball movie, all of which will bring you to tears, or close. Which is ironic, as Dan points out, since a notable line from that movie is "There's no crying in baseball".

And, even though as a family we live for Notre Dame football, baseball perhaps occupies an even higher rung on that ladder. We have bled Dodger blue since we were kids, following the fortunes of Don Drysdale and Maury Wills, Don Sutton and Willie Davis, Garvey, Cey, Sutton and Lopes, Orel Hershiser and Mike Scioscia. We can tell you where we were when Fernando Valenzuela threw his no-hitters, and of course, when Kirk Gibson hit his meteoric homerun to beat the A's in the first game of the '88 World Series. That day was one of the best sports days in our family history; on that day Notre Dame upset Miami

31-30 on their way to an undefeated season and the national championship (we watched the clinching fiesta Bowl victory in Tempe, and Dan and I even made the highlight film, thanks to our good seats). The first time my dad took us to a game at Dodger Stadium, seeing the field was like looking down into the Grand Canyon; it just spread out deep and wide and green, before us, the players puny against its vastness. But some of my best Dodger memories are just being in my bedroom, and hearing Vin Scully's reassuring voice narrating a Dodger game from a transistor radio my dad was listening to as he worked in the garden outside my bedroom window. That is the sound of summer.

In 2010 I finally made it to Pittsburgh, where Roberto Clemente is immortalized.

What is it about baseball that evokes such passion, such nostalgia? More than any other sport, why does it take us back? Is it because it is paced and laconic, with plenty of time to think and ponder and socialize between pitches? Is it because it has a history, with heroes of mythic proportions, and indelible moments of legend? Babe Ruth calling his homer. Lou Gehrig's farewell speech. Bill Mazeroski's shot heard round the world. Jackie Robinson stealing home. Willie Mays catching a fly on the dead run, over his shoulder, then spinning and launching a throw back to the infield. Roberto Clemente, with his rocket of an arm, rifling the ball to nail a runner at third. Baseball lends itself well to stats, and some of these numbers are just burnished in bronze. Babe Ruth's 714 homers, Hank Aaron's 755, Roger Maris' 61; Clemente's 3,000-hit lifetime total. Ted Williams' .406 season average.

I was not immune to collecting heroes. The only two baseball cards I still have are Roberto Clemente and George Brett, the latter hailing from El Segundo, a contact hitter and the last player to flirt with a .400 season average (he hit .390 in 1980). Brett's poster, which I have had since I was a kid, hangs in my classroom. And Clemente – he was my childhood baseball hero, maybe because he was everything I was not, as a ball player. One of the first great Latin ballplayers (he hailed from Puerto Rico), Clemente hit for both average and power, had a cannon for an arm, and was maybe the best all-around right fielder of all time (yes, I know, Babe Ruth played right field as well, but Clemente was a better fielder). And he played the game with passion and aggression. Moreover, he was a great humanitarian. He died in 1972 when a plane he had chartered to bring supplies to earthquake-ravaged Nicaragua crashed shortly after takeoff from Puerto Rico. If I wanted to be Jack Snow in football, I certainly wanted to be Roberto Clemente in baseball.

And the dad thing is totally connected to baseball. Just watch Field of Dreams or The Natural: all a kid wants to do is play catch with his dad, and, once grown, he or she will return to that memory for years. Cathy shared a special bond with her dad over the beloved Cubs, whom Jack never saw in a World

Series; he died in 2012, before the Cubs won it all in 2016. I took the girls to Dodger games annually, telling them, as we drove through the turnstiles, that Dodger Stadium was their second home and would always be there for them (it won't, but that's beside the point).

Left, two of the staunchest Cub fans I know: Cathy and her Dad, Jack Schwemm. Right: Bridget, like Carrie, was an early and regular visitor to Dodger Stadium.

My dad would take us over to the fields at Center Street School to pitch to us, and I particularly remember him doing that for my sisters, who were good softball players. We played Little League and Babe Ruth and Bobby Sox, marching in the annual baseball parade which kicked off spring-summer baseball season in El Segundo. Katie was Little League Princess one year, which meant she rode in a convertible in the baseball parade, and got a kiss from big leaguer Ken Brett.

Dad took us to Dodger games every year, and Dan remembers two in particular. In one, Willie Crawford hit a home run into the left field pavilion, where we were sitting, in the ninth to win it for the Dodgers. In another game, against the rival Giants, we sat in reserved level on first base side. Willie Mays, one of the game's all-time greats, came up to bat at the end of the game with men on base. Sitting near us was an elderly, blind Black man in a Giants cap, listening to the game on a transistor radio. "C'mon, Willie", he screamed into the radio.

In 1968 Terry and I (back row) played for the minor league Yankees.

Dad was involved in our Little League, where he kept official score and even announced games (my dad! At the mic!), an enviable job for which you sat at the front of the snack bar. Mom worked the snack bar at times, handing out snow cones and hamburgers and hotdogs, Pixie Sticks (pure sugar), and sour orange gum, which we chewed during the game. Retrieved foul balls were rewarded with a snow cone, and the best snow cones were those customized by asking for a number of flavored syrups.

Dad didn't coach; that was the domain of long-standing older men, absolute institutions, some of whom were tyrants and/or drunks. Though, to be fair, many were not. Dan remembers that Dad filled in as manager for his team when the regular manager was out of town. Dad. As coach, definitely did not show favoritism toward his son. Dad sat Dan on the bench for the first three innings, after which he had Dan playing outfield and batting toward the end of the lineup.

For a while, baseball was life. We played baseball in the backyard, pickle in the front and back, whiffle ball in the driveway, and over-the-line at Center Street. We would pitch to each other at Chevron Park, at Thompson Field on the west side of town, and in the batting cages at Rec Park. We played over-the-line with Uncle John in Worcester. Baseball was an integral part of growing up, for us, and likely for many others. The memories are good; baseball continues to take me back to a simpler time. And maybe even more. In Bull Durham, Annie quotes Walt Whitman: "I see great things in baseball…it will repair our losses and be a blessing to us."

Southwestern Skies

Our return from the East Coast always took us through Springfield, bonus time to visit PaMac and Aunt Carol and my cousins. When we left there it was with a sense of finality. See, we kids didn't know if we'd be doing this again; we didn't, to my knowledge, plan to make a driving vacation across America every several years. This could have been just a one-off. And when we left Springfield for the second time on a trip, it could have been with that whole "return trip" letdown; we had been there and done that, and now we were just on the way home. In 1969 we went back the northern route, I80 through Iowa and Nebraska, and I don't recall much from that route: it was flat and boring but you could make good time on the highway. The other three times we retraced our path through the Southwest. Although it was ground we had covered before, our stops were different on that way back. And they were stops at locales that, in future years, would become very important to me. It was on these trips that I began a lifelong love affair with the Southwest, its skies and landscapes, its cultural and natural history, its original inhabitants and their material culture. Navajo rugs grace my walls and Hopi kachinas sit on my bookshelves. I studied in the Southwest. I worked in the Southwest. I got married in the Southwest. But first, we drove through Oklahoma.

Which was nondescript. But beautiful and bucolic, in its own way. Then on to Texas, again, but just the panhandle; I would not see any of the rest of Texas until years later. Then I would see a LOT of Texas. Kayci and I got our first permanent jobs with the Park Service in San Antonio in 1985, at San Antonio Missions National Historical Park. No doubt you've heard of one mission in San Antonio: the Alamo. There are actually four others, all strung like pearls along the San Antonio River from its headwaters in what is now downtown San Antonio, then south out of town on its way to the Gulf of Mexico. The NPS manages those four missions as part of a relatively recently-established national park, and in a unique setting: those missions are all active Catholic parishes, serving their respective neighborhoods in south San Antonio. Which means that as I worked the visitor center at Mission Concepcion on a Sunday morning, parishioners would file in on their way to Mass. We Rangers became part of the parish, really. Separation of church and state? A little blurry here. We were invited to join in the post-Mass menudo (locally known as a breakfast of champions and a hangover cure, the tripe in that stew is something to deal with. Tripe seems to get bigger as you chew it).

The Alamo, the first of those missions along the river, is decidedly NOT in the national park. The Alamo is owned by the state of Texas and is not an historic site per se; it is a "state shrine". Get the religious connotations? It is the spiritual center of Texas, part of that state's creation myth, which is mostly true, as far as I can tell. The heroes of the Alamo, those brave Texans who died in 1835 defending it from Mexican General Santa Anna, are revered as saints in that state. Jim Bowie. Davy Crockett. William B. Travis. And the Alamo itself is run by the Daughters of The Republic of Texas, whose defense of the Alamo is no less relentless than that of the original Texan defenders. I would say the National Park Service never stood a chance of gaining the Alamo.

**Mission Concepcion at San Antonio Missions NHP, where I wore the
Ranger hat for the NPS. Did this count as going to Mass?**

I found Texas to be a world unto itself. It was at one time,
unlike most other states, its own nation (or so they thought) and
there may be many Texans who still think that it is. I thoroughly
enjoyed my time there. San Antonio was lush and warm, more
like East Texas and Louisiana, and not at all like the panhandle
or the arid desert of West Texas. Kayci and I drove to see Big
Bend National Park, in West Texas, once; we drove all day, and
we were still in Texas. We visited the Hill Country, around
Austin, home of Texas bluebonnets and other spring wildflowers,
and the LBJ ranch. We floated the warm rivers around San
Antonio and drove down to the gulf coast and Corpus Christi,
where Padre Island National Seashore is located. The food and
the culture of the area were fascinating, and enjoyable. We ate

fajitas for the first time there, before they became more common nationwide.

Professionally, San Antonio is where I made the jump from naturalist (an interpretive Ranger) to biologist. Back in the day there were very few biologist positions in the NPS, and so my first jobs were as naturalists. A natural resource specialist position came open while I was at San Antonio Missions, and I moved into that position. As such I began a bird study on the former agriculture lands of the missions, tracked water quality and riparian function on the portions of the San Antonio River that wound through the park, dealt with park pests such as fire ants and the occasional raccoon or snake that wound up in the mission buildings. It was fun, but not enough. In 1987 a biologist position came open at Death Valley, and I took it.

Land of Enchantment

Returning from Springfield on our cross-country trips, we passed again through the Texas panhandle and into New Mexico, and our timing allowed us to stay overnight in Albuquerque. We ate dinner at a restaurant in Old Town Plaza, La Hacienda, that we found remarkable. It had a tree growing right in the dining room! And a plate glass window looking into the kitchen, where you could watch them making tortillas, and sopapillas. The latter immediately became a family favorite: a simple dough that puffed up when deep-fried, you tore it open and filled it with honey or honey-butter. It's more like a dessert, really. We liked it so much that Mom started making them at home, in her trusty electric skillet, to go alongside chorizo and Spanish rice (topped with sliced avocado, our first exposure to that. Avocado toast was decades in the future). New Mexican food is unlike anything found elsewhere in the country. Chiles are grown here, and the green chiles from Hatch are to die for. Harvested in fall and roasted, they are the complement and even the basis for many dishes. I still make green chile posole (hominy) stew, and I bought a deep fat fryer solely to make sopapillas. Serve both at my Christmas party. Whenever I visit New Mexico, I tend to eat the regional dishes until my system cries, no more. It's worth it.

Like some other places, I ended up spending considerable time in New Mexico, down the line. Kayci and I were married in Santa Fe in 1984. Kayci was, at that point, from Santa Fe, where her dad, John Cook, who had moved around the country with the NPS, was regional director of the Park Service's Southwest Region. He had previously been regional director in Alaska, when many of that state's massive national parks had been established by President Jimmy Carter via executive order (the Antiquities Act), and so John had dealt with considerable controversy. And some hardship: one Alaskan winter, they couldn't get tonic water, and ended up drinking their gin straight. John never went back to tonic water; he drank his gin straight for the rest of his life.

Dressed to the nines for my wedding, lids included.

Kayci and I got married on Bastille Day, a French holiday fittingly having something to do with prisons, at the small church of San Isidro (patron saint of farmers). When the priest welcomed the guests to New Mexico (many had arrived from out of state), my grandmother, Nana, turned to my aunt and said, famously, "Pat! We're not in New Mexico, are we?".

The wedding turned out to be a rollicking affair. One of the bridesmaids ended up spending the night in a public park, in a tent with the wedding photographer. And this was maybe the first family wedding at which the Notre Dame fight song, the Victory March was played – as a dance song. The reception was at the historic La Fonda Inn on the Santa Fe plaza, and I would venture to say that of the three elements comprising the reception crowd (family, Notre Dame buddies and Park Service), none were afraid to have a drink. Although at one point, as a friend was buying me a shot of tequila, Mom appeared at my elbow. I mean, she appeared out of nowhere, she apparated, like our Lady of Guadalupe or something. She was all-seeing, and all-knowing. "Tim," she said. "You really don't want to do that." Actually, Mom, I do.

But the kicker came after the reception was over. Kayci's parents had booked us a room at another nice hotel, and we arrived there after the party was over, tired and a little buzzed from the big day. We opened the door, and entered a small room, which led to a larger room. That had nothing in it. Nothing whatsoever. Completely empty. In my buzzed state, I thought, "This is great! This is the foyer, and it's huge. The room itself is going to be fantastic!" We walked around another corner, and all the furniture was in there. It was the bathroom. Every piece of furniture had been piled in there. The headboard had been torn from the wall, the paintings ripped from the walls, the fixtures as well. We had been pranked by – someone. It was more than we could handle, in our fragile state. We were upset, and went back to Kayci's parents' room; They had paid for our room, and were upset as well. Some late-night phone calls ensued. We got another room from the management of the hotel, who were also upset that the room had been damaged, and wanted to press charges against whoever had done this. Now, who had done this dastardly deed? To this day, I'm not sure. Another cold case, waiting to be taken up by an enterprising detective. All we know is this: my brother Terry and childhood friend Dena had posed as Kayci and myself, and gained access to the room. But who did the deed? My ND buddies, and Dan, claim they were drinking at that time and so were not involved. May have been some NPS friends. Apparently, there are pictures of the deed, taken by Dennis (who is without a doubt the nicest of the Coonans, hands down, and is not at all blamed here) and which I HAVE NEVER SEEN. Some things will be taken to the grave, I guess.

The crime of the century, still unsolved, occurred in this unassuming Santa Fe hotel room.

My mom always thought that this incident got our marriage off to a bad start. Not true; now it's just a good story. And it was the first of several Coonan weddings at which the authorities were involved.

I saw a lot of northern New Mexico in my time with Kayci. We attended Pueblo dances, explored the Sangre de Cristo mountains, saw the pueblo at Taos and the miracle church at Chimayo. You can see why Georgia O'Keefe loved it here, and how it inspired her art. Spare land and big sky, as backdrop to striking natural images: cow skulls and desert prairie flowers. Santa Fe was the center of all this. The soft rounded adobe buildings, wooden vigas, sunny courts, blue doors and red flowers. Corner fireplaces. Luminarias at Christmas. When we visited Kayci's parents we would prowl the Santa Fe plaza, soaking up native American art and New Mexican food. Even today my everyday dinnerware is a Mimbres design from Santa Fe, my flatware is Taos. Navajo rugs and sandpaintings, Hopi kachina dolls, Pueblo pottery. Check. The Southwest stayed with me, too.

The River That Cuts Through Time

Flagstaff is not a full day's drive from Albuquerque (at least not for us of the standard 8-hour, 500-mile driving day) but if you visit the Grand Canyon first, it is. And that's exactly what we did, in 1976. Our stop there was fairly brief, just an hour or two on the canyon's South Rim; we did not have time to hike down into the canyon. But not only did this visit allow Mom and Dad to check that off their list of parental required elements (like I said, you HAVE to show your kids the Grand Canyon), it was another life-changing stop. At least for me.

At the Grand Canyon, Mom nervously kept a close eye on Dennis, and I pondered a career in the National Park Service (or, how long until dinner).

First of all, it just blows you away, when you first see it. You catch glimpses of it from the car on the approach, but when you finally walk up to the overlook, up to the wholly inadequate stone walls built by the Civilian Conservation Corps, the canyon just drops out of the sky in front of you, vast and deep, like...Dodger Stadium. You are overwhelmed by its sheer size, variegated canyon stretching all the way to the horizon in every direction. The Colorado – the mighty Colorado River – can barely be seen at the bottom. At the very least, I was certainly awed by it. And of course, I had HEARD of the canyon, and its size, before my visit; can you imagine stumbling upon it, like Coronado's soldiers did in the 1500s, looking for the Seven Cities of Gold? What the fuck? Nothing like this in Spain!

**I visited the canyon with Dennis (left) and Action (middle) in 1982.
Dan visited me when I was there in 1986 (right).**

We did the typical kid things; look Dad, I can throw a rock a mile (the canyon is famously a mile deep). Mom, watch me spit a mile! We peered over the woefully inadequate stone walls into the depths. If Mom had been nervous about us at Niagara Falls, she was even more so here, especially with Dennis, who was known to climb everything.

I'm pretty sure I wanted more of this place. And I got it. If Dan has seen Springsteen three dozen times (and he has) then my record with the Grand Canyon is comparable. I visited numerous times, and spent much time here courtesy of the National Park Service, which has a training center on the South Rim. It's the Horace Albright Training Center, named after the legendary second director of the NPS. Pretty fitting that a national training center should be here; Grand Canyon is the preeminent national park in the Southwest, and even rivals Yellowstone and Yosemite in the West. Definitely one of the "crown jewels" of the system, as they say.

As impressive as the Grand Canyon is from the rim, hiking into the canyon's vastness is a singular and humbling experience.

My longest stretch at the canyon was a six-week stay in 1986 for a "Ranger Skills" course at the canyon, during which we learned rappelling and other far more practical skills (people management, for example). With ample opportunities to explore, I did a three-day hike into the canyon, all the way to the bottom, along some lesser-used trails, and it was a total immersion experience.

The canyon, produced over time by both uplift and river cutting, documents the history of the earth in layers; the bottom layer, or basement rock, is almost 2 billion years old (one of two numbers I make my students learn is the age of the earth – and the solar system: 4.5 billion years; the other is the age of the universe). A descent into the canyon is thus a trip back in time. A lot has happened in those 2 billion years, no? Most of it, biologically, in the last 500 million years.

Over the years, I have spent much time on the Bright Angel Trail, the primary trail descending into the canyon from the popular South Rim. The mule trains ply this trail as well, and that is endlessly entertaining. They plod along, pooping at regular intervals, oblivious to their rider or to the depth to which rider and mount might plunge. Many tourists also head down the Bright Angel in summer, maybe going as far as Indian Gardens (a lush spot; various springs punctuate the trail) or Plateau Point overlooking the Colorado, before turning around for the return uphill trip, which takes twice as long. Some continue to Phantom Ranch, at the bottom, and spend the night. From there, the North Kaibab heads up the other side of the canyon, to the less-crowded North Rim, which is 1,000 feet higher in elevation than the South Rim. The South Kaibab also heads down to Phantom Ranch, and then one can head back up the Bright Angel. For the big hike in 1986 we took the much less-traveled Tanner and Hance Trails, and we needed cramp-ons near the rim due to snowy conditions (it was February). A few years later I spent a weekend hiking down to super-scenic Supai Falls, through the Havasupai reservation.

Cath and I took the girls to see the Grand Canyon when she was working in Flagstaff.

Did Cath and I show our girls the Grand Canyon? You bet. It's the law; you have to do that. Cath was working in Flagstaff, within spitting distance of the canyon, and we took them there in 2010. What effect did that have on them? Not sure. But maybe like Catholicism, it will kick in later.

Mountain Town

On the 1976 trip, we spent the night in Flagstaff, our last night on the road. Flagstaff is a mountain town, elevation about 7,000 feet, a fact Terry and I became painfully aware of that evening. Dad had checked us into a motel on Flagstaff's main drag, the original and historic Route 66, which winds its way east-west through the town. To the north of this begin the hills that eventually lead into the high country. That summer, before our senior year in high school, Terry was training for fall football season; I was training for cross-country. We decided to go running. Up the hills behind our motel. That little run kicked our asses, and was my first practical lesson in altitude: the air is thinner up here. Take it easy.

Four years later, I spent another night in Flagstaff, on the way back to southern California. I was returning from Notre Dame after finishing my junior year, driving back with another southern Californian. At that point I was unsure of what my plans might be after graduation, and I was thinking, in a general sense, about grad school. I knew I was not done yet studying biology, that I wanted more. I think I had forgotten how much I liked Flagstaff, until I drove through it again. And I know I wondered, how is Northern Arizona University, as far as grad programs in biology? Because I knew I'd like living there.

Turns out NAU was very strong in biology. It was of course strong in forestry, with its proximity to the extensive ponderosa pine forests surrounding the Peaks; NAU had an experimental forest on the road north to the Grand Canyon. And the separate biology department was strong in vertebrate (bird, mammal, herp and fish) biology, and in ecology. Perfect. That senior year I only applied to two grad schools: NAU, and UC Santa Cruz; where I didn't get in; I would've gone directly into a PhD program studying whales and dolphins. Which would have been a blast. But no regrets, I gladly went to NAU.

In August 1981 I drove out to Flagstaff – in a rented car; I didn't as yet own one. I had rented a place, sight unseen; a trailer, or half of one, in a trailer park on the west side of town, not far from the university. And hard by the railroad tracks that ran into town. See, Flagstaff is a railroad town, and a road town. Its original history as a transportation hub was built by the trains that hauled timber from the forests and cattle from the rangelands, and was then surpassed by Flagstaff's position on the Mother Road, Route 66, linking the Midwest and the West. Huge freight trains, more than 100 cars long, would pull into Flagstaff, their horns sounding before they crawled through the town itself, crossing several roads, and tying up traffic, as they did so. But the sound of the trains never bothered me. I like trains, consider them romantic, even. To me the rumble and horns of the freight trains are the sounds of the West (granted, the other well-known sound of the West is the call of the red-tailed hawk, very much overused in Western movies).

There was plenty to see and do in and around Flagstaff. Besides being the closest decent-sized city to the Grand Canyon, from Flag one can head down Oak Creek Canyon, south of town, where a popular swimming spot, Slide Rock, is heavily used during the warm months. At the mouth of Oak Creek Canyon sits red rock, new age Sedona, where everyone seems obsessed with crystals (I am, too, but for geologic reasons, not energy). Several national park sites lie near Flag, including Wupatki and Sunset Crater east of town, and Walnut Canyon, to the southeast. Sunset Crater is a cinder cone, a small example of the volcanic forces that pushed up the nearby San Francisco Peaks.

The San Francisco Peaks rise dramatically above the parklike ponderosa pine forest around Flagstaff.

Man, I loved the Peaks. They are what's left of an ancient volcano; the individual peaks of Humphreys, Fremont and Agassiz surround a bowl-like caldera, the sunken remnants of its last eruption. It's high country for sure. Ponderosa pines predominate around Flagstaff itself, and give that town its mountain feel. I loved having tall ponderosas right in town. As one goes up in elevation, the pines give way give way to spruces and firs, and even alpine vegetation at the top, above the tree line (Mt. Humphreys tops out at about 12,600 feet). Along the way are beautiful stands of aspens which turn bright yellow in the fall, and subalpine meadows. And it gets pretty cold up there, something I discovered while on a NAU plant ecology field class. My ND sweatshirt just didn't cut it up there. A ski area, the Snow Bowl, sits on the side of Mt. Humphrey. I skied there once, when Cathy was living in Flag and the girls and I visited. I have been on skis maybe half dozen times in my life. It's not pretty. Just ask my kids.

At the bottom of Mars Hill, a spaceship-themed playground; at the top, an observatory.

The Peaks are also sacred ground, literally, for the Navajo. There are four sacred peaks that demarcate the land of the Navajo, and the San Francisco Peaks comprise one of them. The Navajo reservation, the largest in the country, starts just north and east of town, and so Flagstaff is also a gateway into the Navajo reservation. And it goes both way; NAU had quite a few Navajo students. And my path eventually led me from NAU onto the Navajo reservation.

On the '72 trip, we stopped in Flagstaff for lunch on the way out, and my dad took some pics at our lunch spot. Years later, when I lived there, I found that spot again: an old playground with rocketship-themed equipment sitting at the base of Mars Hill. Drive up Mars Hill and you'll find the Lowell Observatory, an old (1894) picturesque observatory in the pines, where Pluto was discovered in 1930. The West, generally, is great for observatories, because there is less moisture and cloud cover, and less light pollution, to obscure the heavens. Like the observatory, Flag's downtown is also old, and quaint, with hotels like the Weatherford and the Monte Vista (the "Monte V"), remnants of a bygone era, and pretty good places to go for a drink. And nowadays the Museum of Northern Arizona is a fairly modern, spacious institution on the road leading out of town toward the Grand Canyon, but back in the day it was housed in a log building on the town's main drag. That building still exists, and is now a bar, the Museum Club (or "Zoo Club", to locals), featuring country and swing music and catering to loggers and cowboys. I once saw a logger dancing with a chair there. And then pretend to have sex with it. Seriously.

Flagstaff was fun. The undergrads drank at Shakey Drake's, a pick-up joint, while the grad students drank at the Latin Quarter, or the Quality Inn (the "QI"). My second year there I moved out of the trailer park and into a downtown apartment with Scott Johnson, another grad student. Scott was a blond Lutheran from Minnesota, who had attended St. Olaf's. Rooming with me, the California Catholic from Notre Dame. Scott introduced me to NPR, Garrison Keilor's Lake Woebegone and Prairie Home Companion, and women vocalists. He had a thing for women vocalists, especially Carly Simon. Scott was a hotshot biologist, studying birds under the master, Russ Balda, who specialized in corvid (crow and jay) intelligence. I was not in the same league at all, but Balda was on my committee and Scott was very influential in my development as a biologist. Scott, who has been a prof at Towson State for decades, made me a better biologist, and I'm grateful for that. "The march of science must go on," he would tell me.

I, too, studied birds at NAU. I had long been fascinated with raptors, birds of prey, but didn't know anyone who was actually working on them. I came to NAU without a specific master's project in mind, and almost chose an aquatic ecology project, because I knew I could pull it off. But a fellow grad student convinced me to study what I really wanted to study. So I picked the smallest raptor in North America, the American Kestrel, because I thought I could handle them and study them in greater numbers than any other raptor. It was also a project I could do on my own.

The American Kestrel, North America's smallest raptor, and my first love (as a biologist).

All raptors display reversed sexual dimorphism: the female is larger than the male. The reason for this is not well-established. One theory held that males are smaller so they can be more energy-efficient when bringing prey items (grasshoppers, small rodents, birds, lizards) to the female when the latter was in the nest with eggs and then young. I decided to investigate whether males fed the nest ("provisioned") more than females, and if males were more energetically efficient: whether they had a smaller "wingloading", that being the body weight supported by their wings.

I always did like to climb trees.

To do this, I needed to observe a decent number of kestrel pairs during the breeding season, and I needed to capture male and female kestrels to determine if there was a difference in wingloading. I constructed 40-plus nestboxes and hung them in ponderosa pines near Upper Lake Mary and Mormon Lake south of Flagstaff. It was a great study area. I had bought a car, a 1972 Pinto hatchback, that had no seatbelts, a fact not noticed by me until I drove it home to El Segundo and proudly gave my mom a ride in my new car. "Tim," she asked, "where are the seatbelts?" Hmm. I guess there aren't any, Mom. Death trap? I was young, then! The Pinto was in somewhat questionable mechanical condition and would not always make it back from the study site. Thank god for the kindness of strangers.

Grad school was tough. You're never assured of success, that your efforts will produce good data. And I was financially strapped. It showed in what I ate – baked bean sandwiches, cream cheese sandwiches – and in what I weighed. I went down to 117 pounds at one point, and my mom was shocked when I went how for the holidays.

The edge habit of the open ponderosa pine meadows was good for kestrels, and a pleasant place to pursue fieldwork.

But looking back, what absolute freedom and autonomy I had. Conducting my own field study, at no one's behest, and working by myself. I loved going down to my study site, hopping the cattle fences and climbing the pine trees. And I had no idea what to expect in the nestboxes. Kestrels are cavity nesters, usually nesting in holes that other species, like woodpeckers, have made. Somewhat to my surprise, seven kestrel pairs actually showed up and nested in my boxes! You couldn't tell this by looking at the box from the ground; I had to climb the tree and open the hinged top. The first time I discovered a female kestrel on eggs in a box, it was like Christmas morning! I also had a couple of robins and a squirrel using my boxes.

That spring and summer I observed the seven nests, with binoculars from a beach chair, to record prey deliveries to the nest. I would occasionally climb the trees to record number of eggs and number of hatchlings. Turns out that in those nests where males made more prey deliveries, there were more eggs, hatchings and fledglings. I looked at wingloading separately. I built a "bal-chatri" trap, a wire cage with fishing line nooses on top, in which I had a mouse (which I named "Helen of Troy", after another notable captive). I would drive the roads on the outskirts of Flag, looking for kestrels perched on fence posts or telephone poles (which they love to do). When I saw one I would drive slowly by and place the trap by the side of the road, then drive away. Much like cats, kestrels can't resist a moving mouse, and the kestrel would get snagged in the trap when it attempted to catch it. This was a blast, as you might imagine. I would place the kestrel in a cage and take it back to my apartment, where I weighed it and measured the area of the wing. Turns out males are lighter and have less wingloading than females, making them more efficient at catching and delivering prey.

A couple of my collaborators in my master's project. I couldn't have done it without them.

The research wasn't earthshattering, but it was fun and I was able to publish some of it later. The real value of a master's project is that you learn to plan and conduct fieldwork, adjust to changing conditions, record and analyze data, and write it up. Science in a nutshell, and invaluable experience. Changing conditions: I was going to do a second year of fieldwork, but very few kestrels came back to my boxes! That convinced me it was time to cut it off and write it up. Which you have to do at some point, in very investigation (just one more year of data...).

Canyon of the Canyons

That second year of grad school, 1982-1983, I was a TA for some classes, and looking forward to my second field season. But the kestrels didn't returned, or at least they didn't returned to my nest boxes. By that time I had met Kayci, fourth-generation Park Service, who had been working summers up at Canyon de Chelly National Monument. I went there with her that summer, 1983, and volunteered for NPS. The following winter I finished my thesis at home in El Segundo (just Nora, Dennis and myself at home!), defended my thesis in late spring, and went back to Canyon de Chelly, this time as a paid employee, a seasonal naturalist, or interpretive Ranger.

Canyon de Chelly cuts through 200-million-year-old wind-deposited sandstone, and its nooks and niches house remains, such as iconic White House Ruin, of the ancient Pueblo Anasazi, whom the local Navajo call the Old Ones.

Canyon de Chelly, and the Navajo Reservation, was a world unto itself. First of all, the Navajo Nation is actually a sovereign nation (like Texas THOUGHT it was), and has nation-to-nation relations with the US. They are their own thing, and they do their own thing, to an extent. For example, the Navajo are on a different time zone than the rest of the state. Arizona, like Indiana, is stubborn and refuses to go on daylight savings time. But the Navajo do. A fact you need to be aware of when you drive onto the rez in the summer!

In 1983 and 1984, when Kayci and I were at Canyon de Chelly, we were some of the few Anglos in those parts. The only whites in the town of Chinle, at the mouth of the canyon, were some teachers, some doctors and nurses from the hospital, and a few of us park rangers. Otherwise it was a sea of brown faces wherever we went, at the grocery store, the laundromat. We were the minority, and that was a valuable experience. We were stared at. Folks would speak Navajo around us. Kayci had spent time there growing up, and she said old Navajo women would touch her blond hair, having never seen anything like that before.

Canyon de Chelly itself is a canyon system, really a confluence of two canyons: de Chelly and del Muerto. The name Canyon de Chelly is somewhat redundant. "De Chelly" is a bastardized form of the Navajo word for canyon, or place within the rocks: tseyi. The Spanish garbled it into chelly (pronounced "shay"). So, canyon of the canyons. Though the canyon sits squarely on the Navajo reservation (the largest in the US), the national monument there was established in 1931 because of the ancient ruins there. In the canyon's caves and crannies can be found cliffhouses of the Anasazi people, who occupied the area from the 300s to the 1200s AD. These same people, whom the Navajo call "the Old Ones", lived all over the Four Corners region, and other examples of their dwellings, some quite extensive and dramatic, are found at Mesa Verde, Chaco Canyon, and other NPS areas.

Kayci's blonde hair was popular on the reservation. Canyon de Chelly is where I first wore the gray and the green for the Park Service.

Before 1000 AD the Anasazi farmed on the canyon rims and lived in pithouses, but by 1100 they had moved into protected cliff dwellings in the canyons, perhaps for defensive purposes. The remains of these dwellings can be spectacular, and even haunting, and many clues to their material culture have been found in them: pottery bowls and shards, baskets, bows and arrows. As we NPS naturalists used to say, the Anasazi ascribed to the CBS diet: corn, beans and squash, though in later years they added turkeys, an important source of protein.

By 1300 AD the Anasazi were gone, all the cliff dwellings abandoned, somewhat abruptly. And it's entirely unclear why exactly this happened, or where they went. This mystery (and who doesn't like a good mystery? A cold case? See "wedding in Santa Fe") adds to the aura of the Anasazi, and makes their story compelling. It's thought that the Anasazi widely dispersed, and ultimately became the Pueblo peoples of the Southwest. Were they chased out by more warlike peoples? Did they flee to more defensible cities in the Rio Grande Valley and the mesas? A prolonged drought plagued the region in the 1200s, and it's entirely possible that it spelled environmental catastrophe for the agrarian Anasazi in the arid Southwest. They had based their lifestyle and livelihood on a climate that ultimately changed, pulled the rug right out from under their feet. Sounds familiar.

The human presence in the canyon was tangible, from the cliffdwellings of the Anasazi (that's Mummy Cave on the left) to the hogans and pastures of the Navajo.

I think Canyon de Chelly is attractive, and unique, for several reasons. First, it's NOT on a grand scale, like the Grand Canyon. It's more approachable, not so overwhelming. From the rim you can see across the mesa that the canyon cuts into, to the Chuska and Lukachukai mountains, and get a feeling for the geology of the area. You can actually see the bottom of the canyon, with the smallish cliff dwellings under the overhangs, streaks of desert varnish leading down the cliff to them. You can see the current inhabitants of the area, the Navajo, living in the canyon as well. Navajo hogans, with their round eight-side walls, dot the canyon, and flocks of sheep graze its wet meadows in the summer. This is a National Park Service unit, like San Antonio Missions, where current human use is part of the landscape. Which is unusual; most national parks don't have this type of use. Like at the missions, this is a portal into the past. Navajo have lived in and around the canyon for several centuries, and Anasazi occupation takes human use of the canyon back several millennia.

We were definitely outsiders here. As Anglos, we treaded lightly; we were guests. I quickly learned to respect Navajo customs and beliefs. For example, Navajo never shake hands vigorously, but merely touch hands. Cool. Navajo avoid pointing; to do so is rude and perhaps even violates a person's spirit. Instead, some Navajo will point with their lips, pursing them in the intended direction. This took some getting used to.

Because Navajo live in the canyon, visitor access is limited. You can hike down into the canyon at White House Ruin, but that's pretty much it. To hike other trails, you need to go with a Navajo guide, or you can take the jeep tours out of Thunderbird Lodge. Driving up the canyon is spectacular, as you experience all the sinuosity of both de Chelly and del Muerto as the canyons unfold before you. We Rangers led hikes into the canyon as well, and these were popular.

We were allowed to hike in the canyon on our days off, so of course we did, all the while being respectful of the canyon's inhabitants. Over the two seasons I was there I explored the canyon from stem to stern, from source to mouth, from the head of del Muerto to above Spider Rock. Some of the Anasazi dwellings were accessible to us the same way they had been to the Anasazi: via hand and toehold trails etched in the sandstone, trails which had been there for almost a thousand years. The larger ruins, such as Antelope House and Mummy Cave, were impressive, though it was hard to imagine them bustling with people and activity, with the sounds of daily life, in their now-quiet and abandoned state. They were somewhat tomb-like, and indeed some remains of the Old Ones are still there. We came across them. It's for this reason the local Navajo do not go in the Anasazi ruins; they are a place of chindi, which is the spirit left behind by the deceased, present in their remains, in the places where they lived, and even in the mentioning of their names. Not to be messed with.

Which brings up an interesting point. Although I am Catholic and that has colored my beliefs all my life, when I was on the Navajo reservation I think I believed in other things, too. Chindi? Perhaps so. The day we visited Mummy Cave we came upon a skull, one of the Old Ones…that night I had some of the worst dreams I ever had (granted, all my life I've experienced colorful and often disturbing dreams). The Navajo also believe in skinwalkers, witches who can transform into animals. There were a few times when, walking back from the visitor center at night, I was keenly aware of everything I saw and heard. And open to other belief systems, other worlds, beyond or parallel to my own, veiled as they might be. As Kayci's grandfather, Meredith Guillet, an early NPS superintendent at Canyon de Chelly, told me, "There are many paths that lead to the top of the mountain."

Life on the reservation was different. For one thing. It was dry; no alcohol was sold on the reservation. At least, not legally. We heard tell of a woman in town, Juicy Lucy, who was a bootlegger. The Navajo reservation is also open rangeland, which means no fences. If you want to keep sheep and cattle and horses OFF your land, you need to build a fence to do that. One had to be careful driving reservation roads, particularly at night.

Kayci and I used de Chelly as a base from which to explore other cultural sites in the Southwest. We saw the huge Anasazi ruins at Cliffhouse in Mesa Verde and Pueblo Bonita in Chaco Canyon. We visited current Pueblo cities; Acoma, the Sky City, and Taos, in New Mexico. We also ventured onto the Hopi mesas in Arizona. The three Hopi mesas have been occupied for a long time, a Pueblo enclave in the middle of Navajo country. Life there feels ancient and unhurried, somewhat set apart from the current time. We strolled respectfully at Oraibi, on First Mesa. I remember seeing a golden eagle tethered to a roof top; the Hopi had special permits allowing them to keep golden eagles in the traditional manner, to use as a source of feathers. We were lucky enough to view a kachina dance, and I saw a kachina dancer give a boy a kachina doll, a tradition ensuring that the next generation learned the important Hopi gods. All of this felt as though we were somewhere else, no longer in the US that we knew, but instead in the landscape and cultures that existed here long before European humans came on the scene.

We also were able to buy native art directly from the artists, Navajo sandpaintings and rugs, even small paintings by Navajo artists. Thus beginning a minor obsession that has never really subsided.

It was all a wonderfully humbling experience, to be the outsider in a land, to be the newcomer, in a physical landscape that dwarfed me and a cultural landscape that predated my own ancestors' presence on the continent by centuries, and even millennia. It was also where I first wore the flat hat, the Stetson Ranger hat, for the NPS, also starting an obsession that lasts through today, and a career. The hat itself is a big deal, and the one I ordered was actually too big. But I didn't want to send it back. So I stuffed Canyon de Chelly brochures in the hatband to make it fit. Those brochures are still in that hat.

You Can't Go Home Again

Actually, you can. And we did. The last day's drive, Flagstaff to El Segundo. Once again we headed west down the mountain, away from my future-beloved Flagstaff and the big trees and pine air and reasonable temperatures.

The country, and our trip, was behind us now, as we drove across high desert-Arizona and then through the white-hot Mojave Desert, where the agricultural inspection station almost didn't let us bring an old Seth Thomas school clock, from my grandfather's school, back into California, for fear there might be Midwestern moths in it (I think they confiscated the plums we had in the cooler). Finally making it to the edge of civilization, of home as we knew it, the southern California urban-suburban sprawl. Which starts around San Bernardino or Riverside. Back home to Dodger baseball, riding our bikes to the beach, the family dog, Coley, our friends, 8 a.m. Sunday Mass at St. Anthony's. Sunday dinner. Sometimes we'd have our last vacation meal, our last gasp, in a restaurant, maybe a Denny's (a restaurant I remember as being darned good, and which did not live up to that memory later in life - like many things) on the outskirts of LA.

Were we changed because of these trips? Undoubtedly. For one, it had been unabashed family time, time away from our home and friends. Us on a mission. We were the closer for it.

And these trips allowed us to remain close to our roots, to our Midwestern and Eastern families, to whom we are still close.

I think these trips opened up the country, and eventually the world, to us. Travel does that. Good for the soul. Makes one more openminded, empathetic. Look, particularly, at where some of us have ended up, geographically and otherwise. Terry has truly been a citizen of the world. Sophomore year in Ireland. Spanish immersion in Mexico, novitiate in Chile. In his human rights work he has inspected refugee camps in the Mideast for the UN and drunk vodka with Russian generals. And made yearly trips to Gettysburg. Dan has crossed the country in his career in athletic administration, truly appreciating living in parts of the country that are NOT El Segundo. Katie, Nora and Dennis have made it a point to introduce their kids to the country and the world, and I think that next generation now has the openness and empathy that comes from extended and curiosity-driven travel.

And me? Now you know some of it. Thirty years with the National Park Service doing my bit, small as it was, to help save these places – these PLACES – "and the natural and historic objects and the wildlife therein" (that's directly from the Park Service's 1916 enabling legislation). Places deemed important in our natural and cultural heritage. Yes, that sense of place first awakened on these trips. I'm humbled to have been able to help with that mission. And I still just want to be outside.

I don't know anyone who now does the kind of thing we did in the 60's and 70's, packing up the kids and driving to the opposite coast, taking a month to do it. But vacation – family vacation – is important and worth time spent away from jobs, homes and friends, a fact impressed upon us, and not by edict or statement, but by experience, this experience. As I like to say, it's good to get away, and it's good to come back. We have carried that forward. In fact, Cathy and I and our own little family, Bridget, Carrie and occasionally Annie, may have been at our best when we were on vacation, when we were showing the kids the wonders of this world. Yes, kids, welcome to the world, and let us be your guide, at least for a while. The Grand Canyon. Washington, DC. Old Faithful, Grand Prismatic Spring and grizzly bears in Yellowstone. London, Paris, Switzerland, Prague. And those girls – now adults – are inveterate national and world travelers. Carrie has surfed in Morocco, studied whales in British Columbia, captured piranha in the Amazon from a bug-ridden rust-bucket of a boat, and explored the Galapagos. Spent her college years in St. Andrews, Scotland. Bridget, like her Uncle Dan, has turned a love of athletics into a career as a collegiate-level athletic trainer, and has crossed the country, in so doing.

Now, much of my life, like the country on that last driving day, is behind me, has receded into the past. The past is a funny thing. "The past is a great place to visit," Hawk tells me, "but you don't want to live there." Am I, like Gatsby, borne ceaselessly into the past? Is there a dock with a green light, across the bay? If anything, the past, for me, is a long hallway, with many doors, some of which I chose not to go through, others of which I looked in, briefly, but then quietly shut behind me. But I will continue to go down that hallway, or at least, look back. Thinking about the doors I went through, and those I did not.

And at the end of that hallway, way back there, what is that? The Golden Dome? Carroll Hall? The Grand Canyon or Dodger Stadium? Nope. Think I got it. It's the orange roof of a Howard Johnson's. Get your trunks on, kids, we're heading to the pool before dinner. Boys! Watch Dennis! Please!

About the Author

Tim Coonan was born during the Eisenhower administration and grew up during the 60s and 70s, a fact which greatly influenced his consistent and questionable sense of hair style. He and his twin brother (who became a priest for a while) were the oldest in a large Irish-Catholic family growing up in southern California, from which their family made the epic family station wagon trips retold in this book. Tim's dad went to Notre Dame, and thus Tim and his siblings grew up as Fighting Irish fans in hostile USC Trojan country, a siege mentality that no doubt affected his decision to leave idyllic southern California for the frozen tundra of northern Indiana, to attend college at Notre Dame (two of his brothers did, as well).

Driving home from ND one spring, Tim passed through Flagstaff, Arizona, a Highway 66 town which he fondly remembered from family road trips, and he decided to attend grad school there, at Northern Arizona University, because, well, it was pretty. This led to a love of wildlife, wildlife biology and conservation, and several summers spent as a ranger at Canyon de Chelly National Monument. The rest, as they say, is history. Tim ended up spending 30 years as a wildlife biologist for the National Park Service, chasing bighorn sheep in Death Valley and getting bitten by island foxes in the Channel Islands. In fact, Tim, along with his ex-wife, wrote the definitive (all right, the only) book about that unique and rare endangered species, the island fox of the Channel Islands.

Tim now teaches science to impressionable Catholic kids in Ventura, which means he has, ironically, come full circle, being a product of 16 years of Catholic schooling himself. Tim has two grown daughters and lives in Ventura, California. Tim has spent most of his life trying to be outdoors, and hates wearing shoes, except when hiking (he also wears shoes when teaching).

Made in United States
Troutdale, OR
10/02/2023

13345120R00104